AMERICAN
WOODWORKER™

WEEKEND
PROJECTS

Rodale Press, Emmaus, Pennsylvania

Printed in the United States of America

Library of Congress Cataloging-in-Publication Data

American woodworker weekend projects.

    1. Woodwork.   I. American woodworker.
TT180.A28   1988   684'.08   88-4432
ISBN 0-87857-769-6   (pbk. : alk. paper)

Distributed in the book trade by St. Martin's Press

2   4   6   8   10   9   7   5   3   paperback

Contents

The napkin holder is not only a great caddy for napkins, but it's real handy if there are youngsters around for a meal. For them it seems one napkin is rarely enough. It also looks great with the set of salt and pepper shakers shown in this issue.

Begin construction by cutting the stock for the two sides. Each consists of two pieces of oak, one strip of walnut and one strip of padauk. One and one-quarter inch thick oak is used in order to resaw for maximum economy. Thinner stock may be used if you do not have access to the 1 1/4″ thickness. Cut one piece of oak to 3½″ wide by 12″ long. Cut a second piece of oak 7/8″ wide by 12″ long. Next, rip a 3/4 to 1 inch thick piece of walnut to 1 1/4″ then resaw it exactly in the center. Repeat the operation for a piece of padauk. Both pieces should be 12″ long.

Check all the joints for a proper fit before gluing. If there is excessive ripple from the planer, belt sand lightly. Laminate all the strips with the walnut and the padauk stripes together in the middle.

When the napkin holder blank is dry, resaw and plane each piece to ½″, then crosscut to 5½″. Dado or rout a ½″ groove ½″ from the bottom of the holder 5/16″ deep perpendicular to the grain. Band saw a gentle curve across the top and a shorter curve at the bottom, leaving flat areas on each side of the bottom for feet. Take care not to enter the groove when cutting this bottom curve. Belt sand the faces and perimeter then drum sand the inside curve. Finish sand the inside surfaces. Use a number 220 grit.

Plane an oak strip a little thicker than the groove is wide. Rip 2″ wide and crosscut the exact width of the napkin holder sides (about 4 3/4″). Belt sand the faces of the floor to fit the grooves exactly then finish sand with number 220 grit. Glue and clamp the floor to the sides. When clamping, position the clamps so that the tops of the napkin holder sides don't bow in. Use small pieces of wood scrap or clamp pads to keep the clamps from denting the sides. Break the edges and finish sand with 220 grit. Rub in a few coats of urethane oil and the napkin holder is ready for a feast.

NAPKIN HOLDER
by Jeff Armstrong

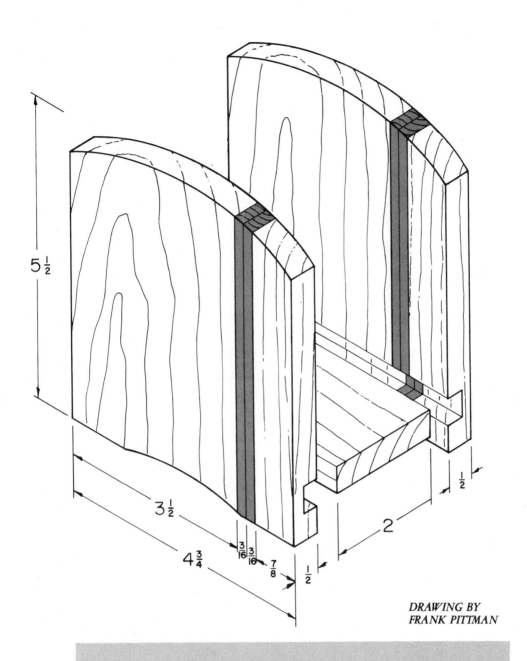

$5\frac{1}{2}$

$3\frac{1}{2}$

$4\frac{3}{4}$

$\frac{3}{16}$ $\frac{3}{16}$ $\frac{7}{8}$ $\frac{1}{2}$

2

$\frac{1}{2}$

DRAWING BY
FRANK PITTMAN

Cutting List for Napkin Holder

Thickness dimensions are for surfaced stock

Oak	1	1¼"	3½"	12"*
Oak	1	1¼"	7/8"	12"*
Walnut	1	¾ - 1"	3/16"	12"*
Padauk	1	¾ - 1"	3/16"	12"*
Oak	1	½" +	2"	4 ¾" +

*Note: Add to the 12" length above the amount of unacceptable snipe anticipated from the planer and adjust to the minimum length the planer can handle safely.

Salt & Pepper Shaker

by Jeff Armstrong

The salt and pepper shakers are a great afternoon project that will help to keep the lady or man of the house more tolerant of the messes you might leave in the basement or garage.

The shakers can be made of any wood combination. For the oak bodies we use walnut and padauk stripes. For the walnut bodies we use oak and padauk stripes.

Begin by planing the oak to 7/8", then rip to 2" and crosscut 9" for every set you will be making. Plane another piece of oak to 5/8". Rip and crosscut the same as above. Rip ¾" or thicker pieces of walnut and padauk to 2". Resaw and plane to 3/16". To reduce tearout, look at the sides of the board and orient the grain at any angle downwards towards the planer. Crosscut 9" and belt sand any extreme ripples or snipe from the planer to insure a good glue joint.

Glue and clamp all the stripes together taking care to keep the sides together and aligned. When dry, rip both sides where there is excess glue. Finish with a 1 7/8" wide shaker blank. A couple of passes on the jointer will work just as well if the grain isn't too wild. Crosscut the salt shaker 4" then crosscut the pepper shaker 4½".

There are two methods to use in counter-boring and drilling the holes for the spice cavity; one when rubber stoppers are used and one for cork stoppers. For rubber stoppers, counterbore with a 1 ½" multi-spur 3/16" deep centered in the bottom. It is a good idea to support the blank on the drill press with a back board and right angle stop to one side. Bore the spice cavity holes with a 1" brad point leaving a full 3/16" thickness at the bottom.

When using cork stoppers for the bottom plugs drill the 1" hole in a piece of scrap then measure the distance the cork sticks out when seated firmly. Counterbore this distance plus 1/8". Drill the spice cavity the same as above.

Draw an S or P on the tops of the shakers no greater in size that the 1" diameter hole. Draw seven equally spaced marks along the S and P lines. Drill through the cavity at these marks with a 5/64" twist drill bit.

Rout the top four edges and the four vertical edges with a 5/16" round over bit.

Belt sand, drum sand and finish sand to 220 grit. Since the salt and pepper shakers will come into occasional contact with food, give them several rubbing coats of urethane oil.

Most large hardware stores have a good selection of corks. The rubber stoppers can be ordered from National Artcraft Co., 23456 Merchantile Road, Beachwood, OH.

6

Cutting List for Salt and Pepper Shakers

1	7/8" x 2" x 9"	Oak
1	5/8" x 2" x 9"	Oak
1	3/16" x 2" x 9"	Walnut
1	3/16" x 2" x 9"	Padauk

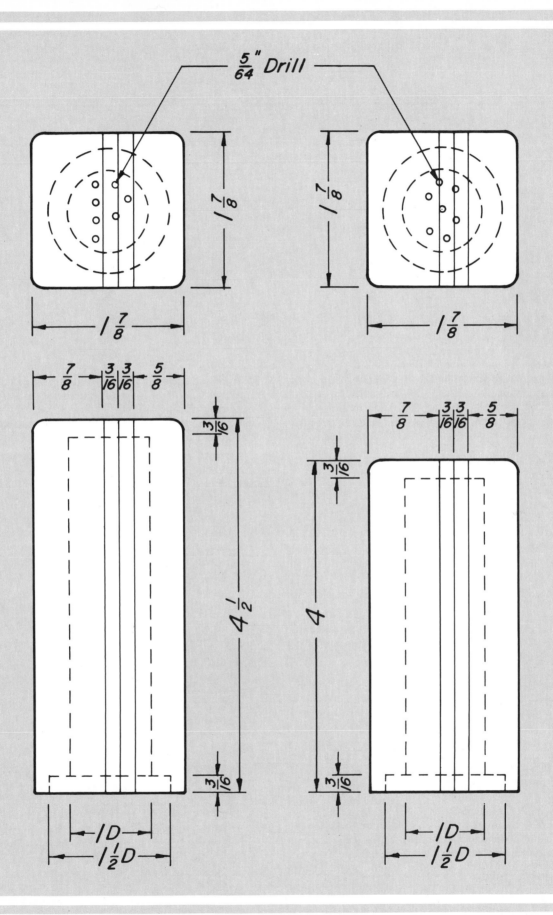

Wooden Basket

by John A. Nelson

The popularity of baskets here in New England is amazing. Every antique shop, every crafts show, every flea market and most yard sales have baskets for sale. Adult evening classes and most colleges offer classes on how to make baskets. Here, in the small New Hampshire town of 5,500 people, where I live, are located two large basket manufacturing companies. Baskets come in all shapes and sizes and are made of all kinds of materials.

This basket is still another style and is made entirely of wood. It can be made of almost any kind of wood and perhaps would be a good way for you to use up some of your scrap. This particular basket can be extended longer than the 16 inch size if necessary. The largest pieces are the ends, part 1, and the bottom, part 2—neither are very large so this project does not require much material. This basket can be made in an evening.

As with any project, look over the plans carefully before you begin so you fully understand how it all goes together and to check that you have enough materials to complete the project.

Start by cutting the two end pieces, part 1, to overall size and temporarily tack the two ends together with two small finish nails. Lightly draw a vertical center line across the top board as illustrated on the detail drawing of part 1. Carefully locate the centers of the four ¼″ diameter holes on both sides of the center line. Measure over from the center line and up from the center line using the given dimensions. Drill the ¼″ diameter holes down through both pieces of wood. Locate and draw the ⅝″ diameter holes on both sides of the center line as noted. Locate and drill a 1⁄16″ diameter hole for the screw that holds the handle assembly in place. It is located on the center line and 9⁄16″ down from the top as illustrated. Drilling the holes with the two parts tacked together insures that both parts will be identical.

Draw straight lines from the centers of the ¼″ diameter holes to form the sides of the basket. Sketch the top surface of the basket, starting from the top center and curving down to the ⅝″ diameter holes on both sides as illustrated. Cut the ends, part 1, with the two parts still tacked together. Sand all edges of the two ends then separate the ends and sand the four surfaces.

Cut the bottom board, part 2, to size per the given dimensions. Trim the two edges with the saw set at 40 degrees as illustrated.

In making the handle, part 3, rough-cut the two pieces and as was done with the ends, part 1, tack them together. Locate and drill the ⅝″ diameter hole through both parts and locate and drill a ⅛″ diameter hole through both parts for the handle assembly. Lay out the outer shape of the handle and cut out. Sand the edges of the two handles with the two parts still tacked together. Keep all edges sharp.

The rest of the basket is very simple—cut all remaining parts to size as noted on the bill of materials and sand all over. Again, keep all edges sharp.

ASSEMBLY

Glue and nail the sides to the bottom, leaving a ⅛″ overhang on both ends. Take care to keep everything square. Glue and nail the side parts, numbers 4 and 5. Line up the sides with the ¼″ drilled holes as a guide. Be careful in nailing the two top side parts in place at the ends as part 1 is a little weak up near the ⅝″ diameter holes.

Attach the handles, part 3, to the bar, part 6, keeping everything square. It is a good idea to temporarily screw the handle assembly to the ends before the glue sets to insure a tight fit.

After the glue sets, remove the handle assembly. Drill four ½″ diameter holes, ¼″ deep into the bottom board as to accept the four feet (plugs), part 7. Glue the four feet in place. Sand all over to remove any rough edges.

FINISHING

Use your favorite stain or paint to finish your new basket, following the manufacturers insructions.

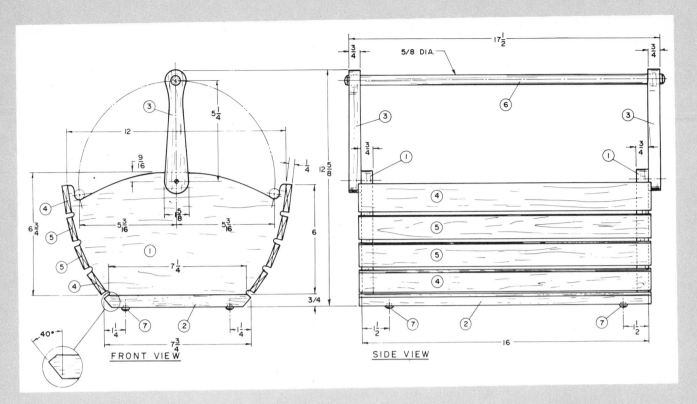

FRONT VIEW   SIDE VIEW

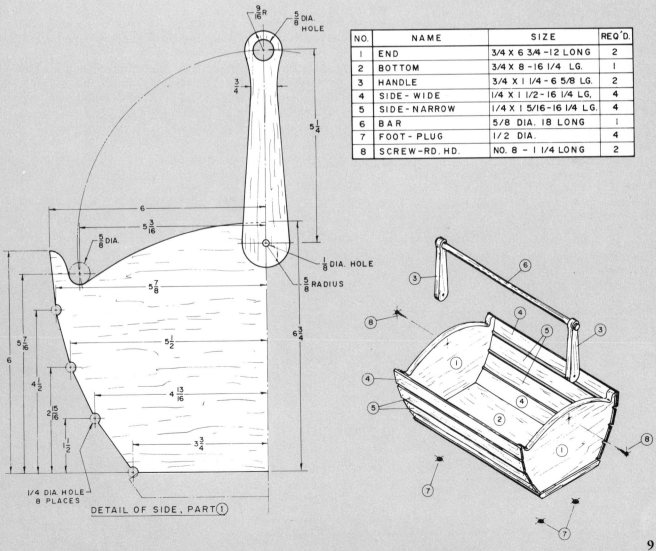

DETAIL OF SIDE, PART ①

NO.	NAME	SIZE	REQ'D.
1	END	3/4 X 6 3/4 - 12 LONG	2
2	BOTTOM	3/4 X 8 - 16 1/4 LG.	1
3	HANDLE	3/4 X 1 1/4 - 6 5/8 LG.	2
4	SIDE - WIDE	1/4 X 1 1/2 - 16 1/4 LG.	4
5	SIDE - NARROW	1/4 X 1 5/16 - 16 1/4 LG.	4
6	BAR	5/8 DIA. 18 LONG	1
7	FOOT - PLUG	1/2 DIA.	4
8	SCREW - RD. HD.	NO. 8 - 1 1/4 LONG	2

9

This is an easy project to build that is not only decorative, but also provides a useful purpose once completed.

The basket requires two pieces of mahogany 1 by 5½ by 14 inches and one piece of oak 14 by 5½ by 2¼ inches. One piece of mahogany is glued face to face on the oak and will be the top of the bread basket. The oval is laid out on the mahogany with a wall thickness of ¼ inch. The inside space is sawn out first. The saw kerf should come in at the end grain and go perpendicularly through the basket wall, then curve over to the line marking the inside wall of the basket. Doing this allows for a good flat gluing surface so the kerf becomes almost invisible in the finished basket. The basket is sawn at a 6 degree angle.

With the inside sawn out, the kerf is glued and clamped with as much pressure as you can muster making sure the figure in the wood lines up exactly. When the glue dries, sand the inside of the basket to the finish stage, then glue the second piece of mahogany on to the bottom of the oak. Be extremely careful about the glue squeezing out to the inside of the basket.

The final step is to saw the outside shape of the basket. With this done the top piece of mahogany is sanded square to the bottom. This gives a top visual edge of about 1/8 to 3/16 inch plus gives a slight change in direction in the profile view, preventing the basket from appearing slab-sided.

OAK AND MAHOGANY BREAD BASKET
by Tom Crabb

PHOTOGRAPH BY THE AUTHOR

A quick finish is salad bowl oil approved by the FDA as a food additive. I don't much like the finish of salad bowl oil so I soaked my basket in re-heated pre-boiled linseed oil. Use a galvanized bucket half full of linseed oil and heat it on the kitchen stove until tiny bubbles begin to show. Then soak half the basket at a time for about 15 minutes each. Don't overheat the linseed oil. The hot oil totally permeates the wood for a stabilizing and water resistant finish. The excess oil is wiped off and the basket given several days to air out before use.

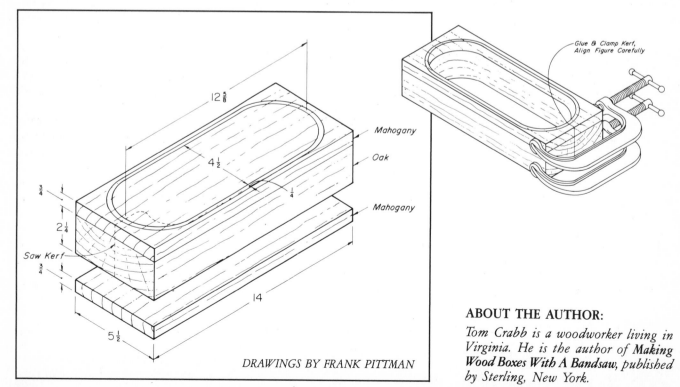

Glue & Clamp Kerf, Align Figure Carefully

Mahogany

Oak

Mahogany

Saw Kerf

DRAWINGS BY FRANK PITTMAN

ABOUT THE AUTHOR:

Tom Crabb is a woodworker living in Virginia. He is the author of **Making Wood Boxes With A Bandsaw,** *published by Sterling, New York.*

Bentwood Shelf

by Dennis Watson

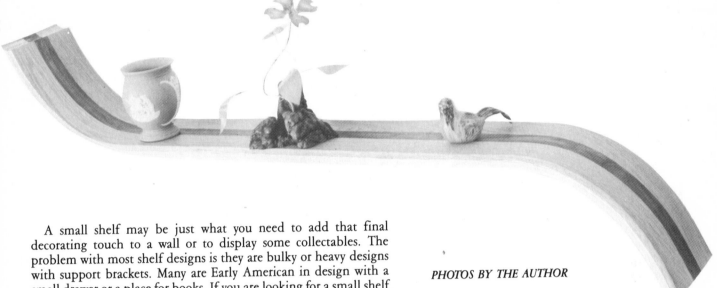

A small shelf may be just what you need to add that final decorating touch to a wall or to display some collectables. The problem with most shelf designs is they are bulky or heavy designs with support brackets. Many are Early American in design with a small drawer or a place for books. If you are looking for a small shelf with clean simple lines, more of a contemporary look, this bentwood shelf may be what you're looking for.

The shelf is laminated to shape; I choose laminating over steam-bending for three reasons. First, the design requires three sections, two from white oak and one from walnut to be bent to shape then glued together. Laminated forms are more precise; that is all three sections should come out pretty close to the same shape, making gluing them together easier. Steam bent forms are not as consistent because two pieces of wood are not identical and will spring back differently. The second reason is that successful steam bending would have required a steel bending strap on the outside of the curve. Since this design has a reverse curve (one end bends up, the other end down), the strap would have to be placed on one side on the left end and the opposite side of the shelf on the right end; joining them together at the middle would have been difficult. The third and last reason is that I wanted to glue all three sections back together. Since the wood was steamed and its moisture content raised, it would have to dry to a lower moisture content before gluing.

Laminating is a simple, straightforward technique that does not require a lot of equipment. The basics are as follows: the wood is cut or ripped into thin sections which will easily bend around the form without breaking; when glued together the strips form an integral board and retains its shape. There is a slight amount of spring back once the clamps are removed, but this is minimal.

When selecting the wood, it's best to pick straight grain stock; figured wood with wild grain will not bend as well. You'll need ten strips finished to 3/32 inch thick. When gluing up the strips they have a tendency to slip, therefore, cut them about ½ to 1 inch too wide and a couple of inches too long.

There are a couple of ways to rip the strips; a 10 inch table saw will easily rip 2½ inch wide strips; the only problem is a carbide rip blade has about a 1/8 inch kerf and wastes a lot of wood. Some of the new thin kerf Japanese blades have a 1/16 inch kerf and therefore will waste less wood. The band saw is your other option. Here again, depending on the blade you select, the kerf will be about 1/16 to 3/32 inch.

Before ripping the strips, mark the stock so you can glue up the strips in the same order as they were cut from the board. This makes the glued up shelf look as if it's one piece of wood, not ten.

Rip a strip of wood just a little oversize then joint the surface of the board and rip another strip (it's easier to joint a thick board than it is to plane both sides of a thin strip). Continue until you've cut a couple of extra strips. After all the strips are ripped, they should be surfaced planed or sanded to remove saw marks on the side that was not jointed.

It's difficult to surface thin strips on the thickness planer. I solved the problem by attaching the thin strip to a carrier board with double back carpet tape. The strip and carrier board were then run through the planer.

With the strips cut and surfaced, the form is the next order of business. The form is made from four pieces of ¾ inch particle board or plywood glued and nailed together. Cut the blanks roughly to shape, then glue and nail together. Transfer the design from the drawing to the form and band saw to shape. Smooth the band saw marks out with a file or sand paper.

Attach the right curved forms to a piece of plywood or particle board base with No. 8 x 1½ flat head screws and glue. Attach the left curved form to the base with screws only. The reason for not using glue on the left form is that the strips are clamped to the straight section, but they must bend away from the straight section around the left form block. If the left form block were rigidly attached to the base there would be a short length of lamination in which clamping pressure could not be applied

BENTWOOD SHELF

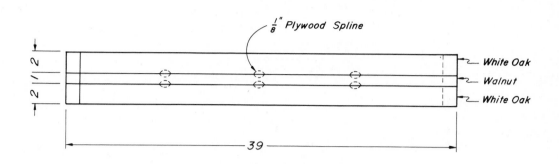

$\frac{1}{8}"$ Plywood Spline

2 1/2

White Oak
Walnut
White Oak

39

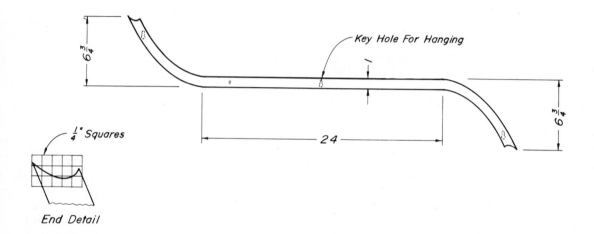

$6\frac{3}{4}$

Key Hole For Hanging

1

24

$6\frac{3}{4}$

$\frac{1}{4}"$ Squares

End Detail

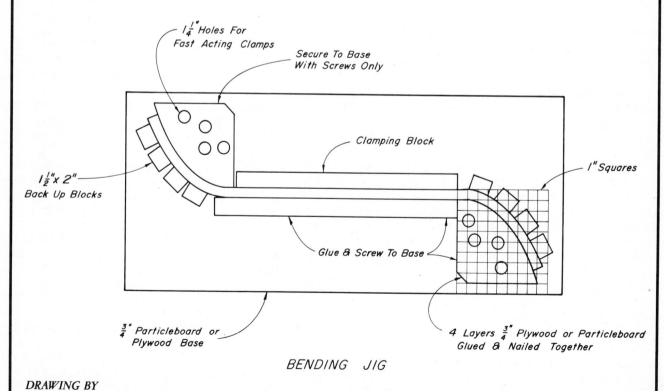

$1\frac{1}{4}"$ Holes For
Fast Acting Clamps

Secure To Base
With Screws Only

Clamping Block

1" Squares

$1\frac{1}{2}"$ x 2"
Back Up Blocks

Glue & Screw To Base

$\frac{3}{4}"$ Particleboard or
Plywood Base

4 Layers $\frac{3}{4}"$ Plywood or Particleboard
Glued & Nailed Together

BENDING JIG

DRAWING BY
FRANK PITTMAN

Glue up the strips in the same order as they were cut from the board.

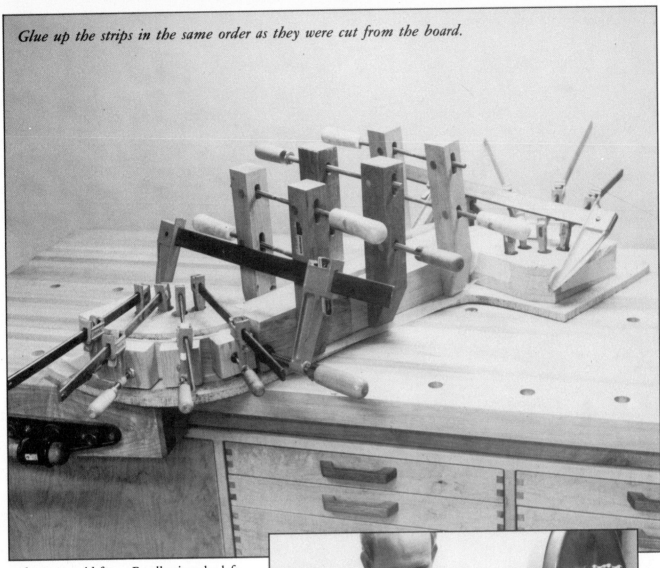

and a gap could form. By allowing the left block a slight amount of ''give'', you can clamp the strips to the straight section then to the left form (see the drawing). The form will actually deflect a small amount and pull the strips up tight. The form, however, is still firmly enough attached to the base to allow the strips to be bent and clamped in place.

Add the straight piece between the two curved forms. For this I used some scrap 8/4 oak glued and screwed to the base.

The laminates are clamped in place with quick acting clamps. To provide a clamping surface, drill 1¼ inch holes in the form. If you use pipe clamps, you'll have to saw a flat face on the opposite side of the form to provide a clamping face.

Now, place the laminates in the form and clamp in place. Place a back up block over the laminates and trace the curve onto the backup block; band saw to shape. Remove the clamps and reclamp using the backup blocks. All the laminates should pull up tight; if they don't, trim the backup blocks until they do.

After laminating, trim each section on the band saw.

13

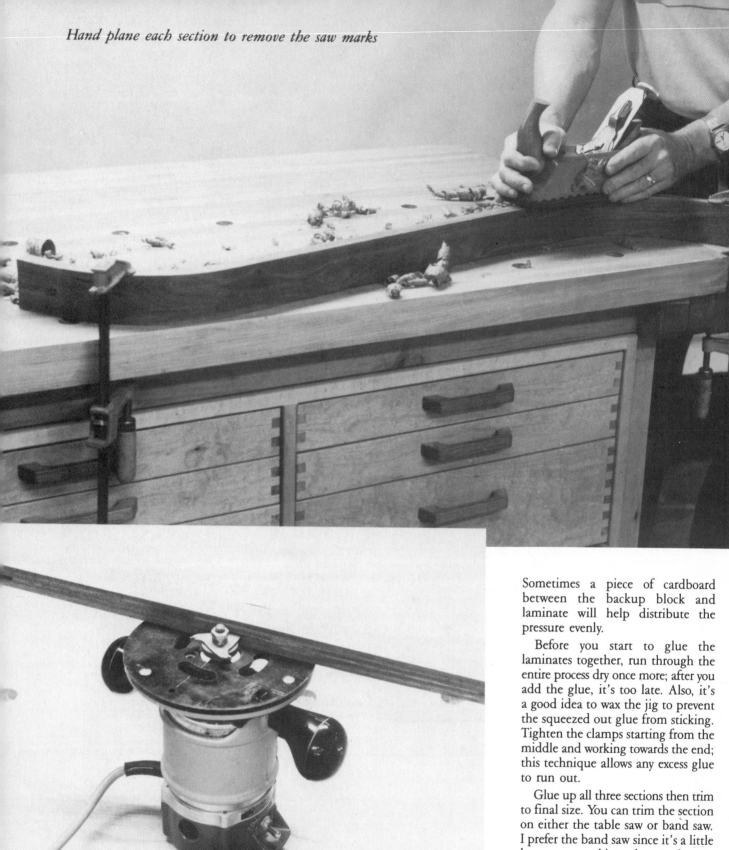

Sometimes a piece of cardboard between the backup block and laminate will help distribute the pressure evenly.

Before you start to glue the laminates together, run through the entire process dry once more; after you add the glue, it's too late. Also, it's a good idea to wax the jig to prevent the squeezed out glue from sticking. Tighten the clamps starting from the middle and working towards the end; this technique allows any excess glue to run out.

Glue up all three sections then trim to final size. You can trim the section on either the table saw or band saw. I prefer the band saw since it's a little less nerve racking than trying to maneuver a bent piece of wood through a saw blade rotating at 5000 RPM. After you have the pieces trimmed up, hand plane to remove the saw marks. Dry fit together to make sure the joints pull up tight.

Cut the slots for the splines

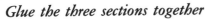
Glue the three sections together

Layout and carve both ends

When gluing the three sections together, they have a tendency to slip and slide a little; dowels or splines help eliminate the problem. I used 1/8 inch splines with the groove cut with a router and slot cutter. On the curved part where I couldn't cut the grooves, I clamped a batten on both sides to align the sections.

After the sections have been glued together, use a cabinet scraper or sandpaper to smooth the surface. Trim the ends square on either the band saw or table saw.

It's a good idea to wax the jig to prevent the squeezed out glue from sticking.

Layout the design for each end then waste the wood with a carving gouge and mallet. Carving marks are easily removed with a surform or file.

The shelf has no visible means of support, no screws or nails; it tends to float on the wall. This is accomplished by routing three picture frame keyholes in the back.

Sand the shelf then finish as desired; I used two coats of Watco Danish Oil, the second coat was wet sanded with No. 600 wet and dry paper. A coat of paste wax completed the project.

When hanging the shelf, the difficult part is to align all three holes with screws or nails in the wall. You can make the job easier, however, by using 3/8 inch dowel centers placed in all three holes. Place the shelf against the wall, level it, then tap the shelf gently to leave a dimple in the wall board at the center of each keyhole. Install the screws or nails and the shelf should slide easily in place.

Use a surform or file to form the final shape of both ends

ABOUT THE AUTHOR:
Dennis Watson is a contributing editor to The American Woodworker.

Bench-Coffee Table

By W. Curtis Johnson

This bench or coffee table is simple in design but extremely sturdy, and is unaffected by wood movement. It uses just six boards and the through mortise and tenon joint. The piece provides an opportunity to use the decorative wedged tenons described in this issue of *The American Woodworker*. The bench pictured here and detailed in the figure is 48 inches long, 16 inches deep, and 16 inches high, and is made of American black walnut. The wood used and the size are not critical, but I find the one-to-one-to-three ratio of the dimensions pleasing.

Begin by selecting the boards to form the top and the legs. It is best if each section can be made from the same piece of lumber so the grain and color can be carefully matched. After trimming the edges of the presurfaced lumber on a circular saw, I smoothed them with my 14-inch jack plane. Each set of edges to be joined was smoothed as a pair, by holding the boards face to face in a vise. This technique works well with a hand plane because the edges need not be truly perpendicular to the faces. The edge of each board in the pair has the same angle and the edges compliment each other as the boards are opened like the pages of a book. I find that edges prepared in this way form a tighter joint than edges prepared on power tools. With care, the glue line will be invisible, and if you have carefully matched the grain, it will appear to be one continuous board. Check to make sure the edges are straight, and then clamp them without glue. For the top, use five clamps about 16 inches apart and alternate them between the top and the bottom of the piece to even the stresses. Three clamps are enough for the leg sections. Make sure that the joints are tight and that the surfaces are reasonably flat. If everything checks out, glue the boards together.

After the glue is dry, you'll need to dimension the top and leg sections. Their faces could be surfaced at your local planing mill, but I prefer to use my jack plane. With walnut lumber and a sharp iron, surfacing is a joy as long, thin shavings curl out of the plane. Relax and enjoy this process. Making the piece should be as important as the finished product.

When these sections are dimensioned to your satisfaction, it is time to remove the semi-circular cut out between each pair of legs. A bandsaw, jig saw, or coping saw will all work here, and a drum sander is more convenient for smoothing the radius than sanding by hand.

The two side pieces and stretcher are simply ripped from a piece of lumber and dimensioned. The side pieces are slightly narrower in the figure and will look better than the ones on the bench I made. Remove the cut-outs on the side pieces.

Now it is time to chop out the mortises. Cut the tenons on the leg sections and the stretcher to fit each mortise. Be sure to mark each piece so you will know which tenon fits which mortise. Cut the kerfs in each tenon, and make the wedges. After checking the fit of each joint, you are ready to glue the stretcher into the two leg sections. Only after this is completed should the leg sections be glued into the top.

The dados in the side pieces that will accept the legs can

The end grain of the through mortise and tenon joints provide decoration without overwhelming the natural beauty of the wood.

now be marked directly from the partially assembled piece. These grooves may be made on the circular saw, with a router, or by hand. Be sure each dado is individually sized to fit snugly on its leg to add maximum stability to the bench. The side pieces are glued to the legs and to the top. All edges are rounded over with a ¼ inch radius except the edges on the top surface of the bench, which are rounded over with a ½ inch radius. Sand the bench smooth and apply the finish of your choice.

BENCH - COFFEE TABLE

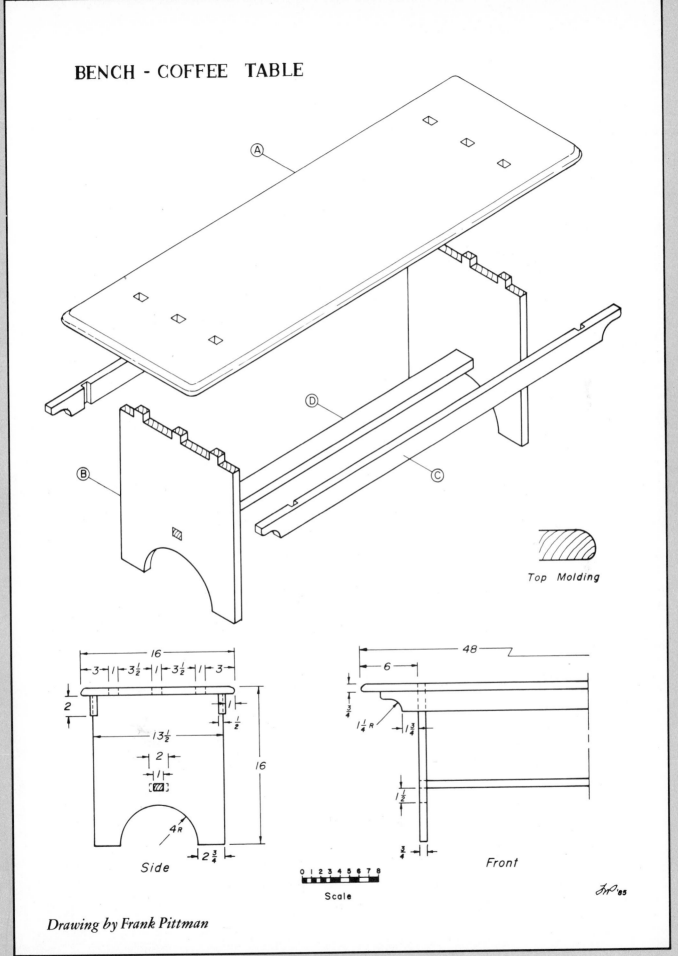

Top Molding

16

3 | 1 | 3½ | 1 | 3½ | 1 | 3

2

13½

2

1

4 R

2¾

Side

48

6

¾

1¼ R

1¾

1½

¾

Front

0 1 2 3 4 5 6 7 8

Scale

JP '85

Drawing by Frank Pittman

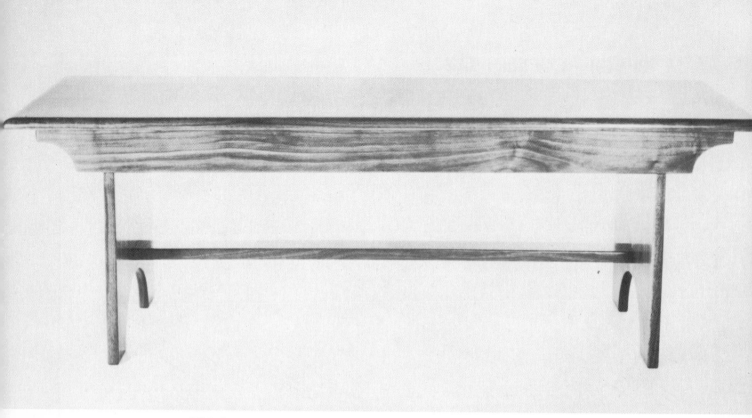

This bench or coffee table uses just six boards and is extremely sturdy.

The wide leg sections are another chance to display the grain of the wood. The cut outs between the legs and at the ends of the side pieces give the piece unity. The mortise and tenon joints are also repeated here.

BILL OF MATERIALS

(A) 1 Top ¾" x 16" x 48"

(B) 2 Leg Sections
    ¾" x 13½" x 16"

(C) 2 Side Pieces
    ¾" x 2" x 44"

(D) 1 Stretcher
    ¾" x 2" x 36"

Dovetail Clocks

by W. Curtis Johnson

There is something special about clocks that makes the construction of their case a favorite project for woodworkers. It is more than the nostalgia of mechanical movements with rotating hands over the silent electronics of digital displays. A clock is ''looked at'' more than any other piece of furniture, so perhaps it is the repeated enjoyment of the lines, construction and wood grain. Clocks are treated gently compared to most furniture, and are an item that is treasured generation after generation.

The clock case described here combines the pleasure of making a clock with a chance to display your dovetailing skills with exposed joints. The dovetail joint ensures a sturdy carcase so this clock will survive to become a family heirloom. For the beginner, there is no better project to inspire learning the art of sawing dovetails. Dovetails are one of the few basic woodworking joints and should be mastered by every craftsman, professional or amateur. Refer to the March 1985 issue of *The American Woodworker* for Franklin Gottshall's description of laying out and making through dovetails. The clock pictured here was my first project using hand cut dovetails.

The clock has clean lines with decoration provided by the end grain of the through dovetail and bridle joints.

Purchase your clock movement before beginning the project. A list of mail order houses that specialize in movements is included at the end of this article. Start by measuring the movement to determine the appropriate height, width, and depth for your case. Not only have movements that I purchased been different from the catalog description, but their dimensions have sometimes been different from those given in the enclosed instructions.

Don't feel limited to the clock size given in the figure. This first clock was designed for our kitchen, but since then I have made numerous wall clocks following this basic design, some as long as three and one-half feet. This simple but flexible design is suitable for any round faced clock, although I prefer the ''Vienna'' type movements which come in a variety of sizes. These may be silent, have a bim bam chime or a gong (my favorite) that sounds the half hours and counts the hours, or have Westminister chimes that play a tune each quarter hour and count the hours. On my large clocks I have increased the width of the door bottom and sides along with the more obvious dimensions. For three and one-half foot wall clocks, the door sides are 1 5/8 inches wide, the door bottom 2 inches wide, and the back 3/8 of an inch thick. Plan the center of the pendulum to be the same distance from the bottom of the door as the shaft for the hands is from the top.

This clock case was made of American Black Walnut. Choose a wood that appeals to you and carefully select the grain for each piece. Notice how the most prominent piece of wood at the top of the door has grain that surrounds and compliments the face. You can probably do a better job of matching the two sides of the door than I did for this early project. Also, a more flamboyant grain would make the case more interesting than the vertical grain I chose for the back of this clock.

The Bill of Materials lists the pieces for the clock case and their full finished size for the kitchen clock pictured here. Cut these pieces from your lumber somewhat larger than you have planned, and dimension them with a hand plane, or a planer and jointer. The back will probably have to be glued up from two pieces. If you can resaw to make a back with the thickness suggested here, then you can book match the pieces that form the wider board. If you are limited to lumber of standard thickness, a ¾-inch back is all right, but you should match the grain of the lumber you are gluing together.

Next, make the dovetail joints that form the basic carcase. Saw the pins on the top and bottom, and the tails on the sides as shown. Gravity is then pulling on the strongest direction. The top of the carcase extends over the door to protect the movement by keeping dust out of the case. With the dovetails complete and tested, rout out a rabbet for the back. This should have a 3/8 to 1/2 inch overlap and be 1/8 of an inch deeper than the thickness of the back to allow for the hardware securing the movement. The rabbet must be stopped for the top and the bottom, and you will have to be careful of the delicate pins. Stop the rabbet early and plan on cleaning out the corners after gluing the dovetails.

DOVETAIL CLOCK

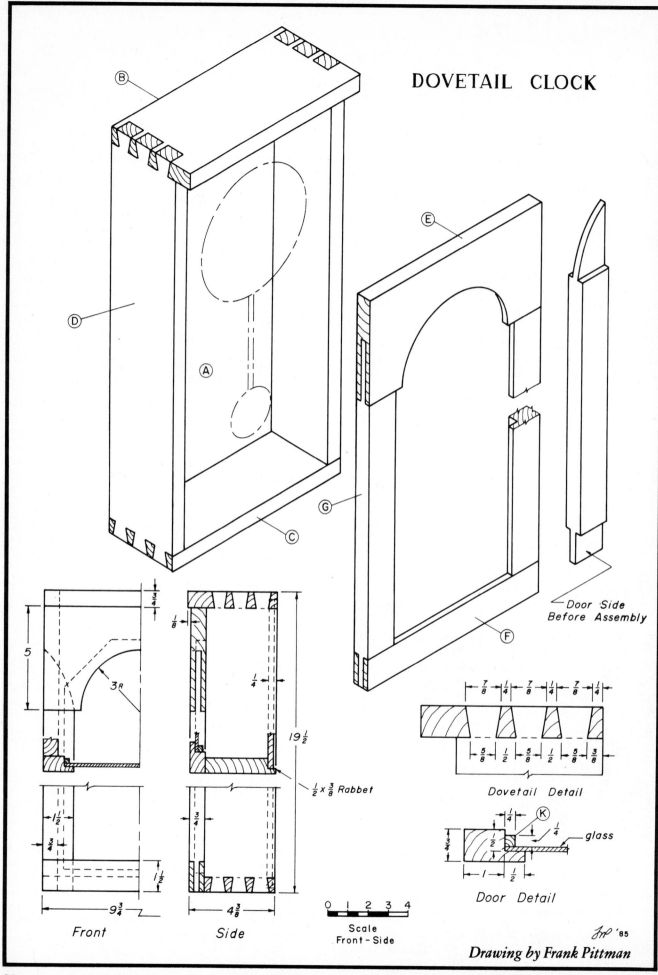

B

E

D

A

G

C

Door Side
Before Assembly

F

$\frac{3}{4}$

$\frac{1}{8}$

$\frac{1}{4}$

5

$3 R$

$19\frac{1}{2}$

$\frac{1}{2} \times \frac{3}{8}$ Rabbet

$1\frac{1}{2}$

$\frac{3}{4}$

$\frac{3}{4}$

$1\frac{1}{2}$

$9\frac{3}{4}$

$4\frac{3}{8}$

Front

Side

$\frac{7}{8}$ $\frac{1}{4}$ $\frac{7}{8}$ $\frac{1}{4}$ $\frac{7}{8}$ $\frac{1}{4}$

$\frac{5}{8}$ $\frac{1}{2}$ $\frac{5}{8}$ $\frac{1}{2}$ $\frac{5}{8}$ $\frac{3}{8}$

Dovetail Detail

K

$\frac{1}{4}$

$\frac{1}{4}$

$\frac{3}{4}$

$\frac{1}{2}$

glass

1 $\frac{1}{2}$

Door Detail

0 1 2 3 4

Scale
Front-Side

Drawing by Frank Pittman

$\mathcal{FP}$ '85

Do all the finish sanding on the inside surfaces of the basic carcase. Then assemble and glue the dovetail joints making sure that the case is square. Clean out the corners of the rabbets and fit the back. Allow about 1/16 of an inch of play for the width of the back to compensate for the extra wood movement across the grain as opposed to the long grain of the top and bottom. The back should be screwed into place to allow for this wood movement.

Measure the case you have constructed and plan the door slightly larger so you can fit it and compensate for any errors. Cut the half circle in the top of the door for the clock face and sand it smooth. I used bridle joints which display end grain that will complement the end grain of the through dovetail joints. These are easily cut by hand, or on a band or circular saw. The March 1985 issue of *The American Woodworker* gives detailed instructions on making a tenoning jig so that you can safely use your circular saw.

Make the mortises in the top and bottom first. Those in the top have the rounded shape of the circular saw blade, since they are stopped after three inches. I used my bandsaw for the remainder of the cuts. Mark the tenons from the mortises. You may have an accurate method for sawing the mortises, but I cut mine a bit oversize and plane them to fit. If you are sawing by hand, knife and remove a chip as described for ends of the pin members of the dovetails before crosscutting the waste from the tenons. The tenons at the top will have to be shaped to fit the circular mortises in the top piece. Assemble the door and continue with the fitting until there are no gaps in your joints. The door should be square and flat.

Glue the door together paying special attention to squareness and flatness. When the glue is dry, fit the door to the case, compensating for any errors. I routed a ½ inch wide by ½ inch deep rabbet for the glass after the door was assembled. The glass could be rectangular or have its corners removed as shown in the figure. Secure the glass with ¼ inch square molding made from walnut lumber and nailed with brass brads. Drill holes to ease the installation of the brads. Use a sharp chisel to form the recesses for the butt hinges, and attach both the hinges and the latch.

The holes for securing the movements should be drilled into the back at this point. Instructions will be included for your particular clock, but before actually drilling the holes, check everything with the entire case assembled. Also, drill the holes for a single hanger at the top and center of the back. The proper position for the beat plaque is determined after the clock with its pendulum is hanging on the wall. Thus, holes for the beat plaque, and a countersunk hole under the beat plaque to help attach the clock to the wall, should be drilled as the last step.

Disassemble the case for final sanding and finishing. Round all the edges. Although simply said, if this is carefully done it may take as long as the entire construction described above. The completed clock should be hung with the hand shaft at eye height. Drill the holes for the beat plaque and use a countersunk screw under the beat plaque to secure the clock in a perfectly level position. I hope your clock will provide you with the same pleasure that mine has provided my family.

ABOUT THE AUTHOR

*W. Curtis Johnson is a frequent contributor to **The American Woodworker**. He lives and enjoys his woodworking in Corvallis, Oregon.*

This kitchen clock has a case of American Black Walnut and a Vienna movement.

Some mail order houses specializing in clock movements are given here. All have catalogs and I have included the details as I understand them. Most of these outlets also sell kits of presawn and shaped lumber for the cases, plans for cases, beveled glass, and hardware:

Craft Products — 2200 Dean Street, St. Charles, IL. 60174; [312] 584-9600. "Clock Builder" catalog $2.00; "Heirloom" catalog $1.00.

Elcraft — P.O. Box 111, Carlsbad, CA 92008; [619] 722-2866.

Emperor Clock — Emperor Industrial Park, Fairhope, AL 36532; [205] 928-2316. Free catalog.

Heinz Jauch — P.O. Box 405, Fairhope, AL 36532; [205] 928-0467. List of items, $1.00.

Heritage Clock — Heritage Industrial Park, P.O. Drawer 1577, Lexington, NC 27292. Catalog $1.00.

Klockit — P.O. Box 629, Highway 'H' North, Lake Geneva, WI 53147; [800] 556-2548. Free catalog.

Kuempel Chime — 21195 Minnetonka Blvd., Excelsior, MN 55331; [800] 328-6445. Free literature.

S. LaRose — 234 Commerce Place, Greensboro, NC 27420; [919] 275-0462. "Keep Book" $2.50.

Mason and Sullivan — 586 Higgins Crowell Road, West Yarmouth, MA 02673; [617] 778-0477. Free catalog.

Newport Enterprises — 2313 W. Burbank Blvd., Burbank, CA 91506; [213] 845-0555. Catalog $2.00.

Turncraft Clock Imports — 7912 Olson Highway 55, Golden Valley, MN 55427; [612] 544-1711. Catalog $2.50.

Viking Clock — The Viking Building, Box 490, Foley, AL 36536; [205] 943-5081. Free catalog.

BILL OF MATERIALS

(A) 1 Back
¼" x 9³/₁₆" x 19"

(B) 1 Case top
¾" x 4½" x 9¾"

(C) 1 Case bottom
¾" x 35/8" x 9¾"

(D) 2 Case sides
¾" x 35/8" x 19½"

(E) 1 Door top
¾" x 5" x 9¾"

(F) 1 Door bottom
¾" x 1½" x 9¾"

(G) 2 Door sides
¾" x 1½" x 16¾"

(H) 1 Molding
¼" x ¼" x 2⅞"

(I) 2 Moldings
¼" x ¼" x 3 7/16"

(J) 1 Molding
¼" x ¼" x 7¾"

(K) 2 Moldings
¼" x ¼" x 13⅞"

(L) 2 Butt hinges
1½" x 1¼" total width

(M) 1 Door latch

(N) 1 Hanger

CANDLE BOX

by John A. Nelson

PHOTOGRAPH BY
DENNIS A. WATERS

In years past, small boxes came in many shapes and forms. They were used to store just about everything. Some had lids that hinged and others had sliding tops. This particular box is an exact copy of an old antique box that probably held candles. Candle boxes often were used to store jewelry and other valuables. This probably offered a great hiding place; who would look for jewelry in a candle box? The original of this box was found in an antique shop in New Hampshire and had a hefty price tag of $325.00.

A box like this is very simple to build, takes very little material, and does not take long to make. After having made eight or ten of these boxes myself, I find everyone who sees them seems to want one. Perhaps I should go into the business of making candle boxes. The actual dimensions can be changed to accommodate almost any size or particular need. Today, they make excellent documentary boxes.

The original candle box was made of maple but could be made of almost any kind of hard wood. They can be stained and finished, or as the original, painted. The original was painted an old powder blue color and was well worn.

Instructions:

Cut 24 inches from the 60″ board for the sliding lid and bottom. Cut into two pieces exactly 5½″ wide x 11 13/16″ long (lid) and 5½″ wide x 11 5/8″ long (bottom). Label the parts and set aside. Then cut the remaining 36″ to exactly 5″ wide x 36″ long. Rabbet the entire length of one edge as shown, 3/16″ deep x 3/8″ wide, per the drawing. Next notch (dado) the entire length of the opposite edge as shown, 3/16″ wide and 3/8″ down from the top edge, (see drawing). Cut the board into four pieces as shown; 12″ long, 5½″ long, 12″ long and 5½″ long. Label them, "right side", "left side" and "ends". Cutting the sides and ends in this order will make the grain pattern "flow" around the box. On one of the 5½″ long pieces, cut 3/8″ off, from the top surface (to bottom of notch) as shown. On the two 12″ long pieces, rabbet both ends as shown. It is important to rabbet thru lip on the front end but do not rabbet thru lip at back end, (see drawing). Be sure to make one side as shown and the other side opposite shown in order to make a left and right hand pair. Then, glue the four sides together with the bottom piece. Nail together with two square-cut nails per joint and along the bottom. Set nails slightly and putty along all joints for a tight fit. Feather the top of the lid by using either a table saw set at 10 degrees or a hand plane, and bevel all four sides of the lid per the drawing. Set the blade of the saw at a height of ¼ inch and, starting in exactly 5/32 inch from the saw fence, cut the flat area in the lid as shown. Cut along the two sides and only one end. Check to see that the lid slides freely within the box without binding. Sand or re-cut the 5/32 inch lip to suit, if necessary. Finally, locate the three finger slots by either carving in by hand with a chisel or drilling in place with a ½ inch Forstner bit on a drill-press set at approximately 5 degrees.

Finishing:

First, sand all over to suit taking care to keep sharp edges at the corners. Next, apply either a stain of your choice or apply paint using an old color. The finish was applied to the outer surface only in the original box. Finally, if the box has been painted, sand all edges slightly to give it that worn, used look.

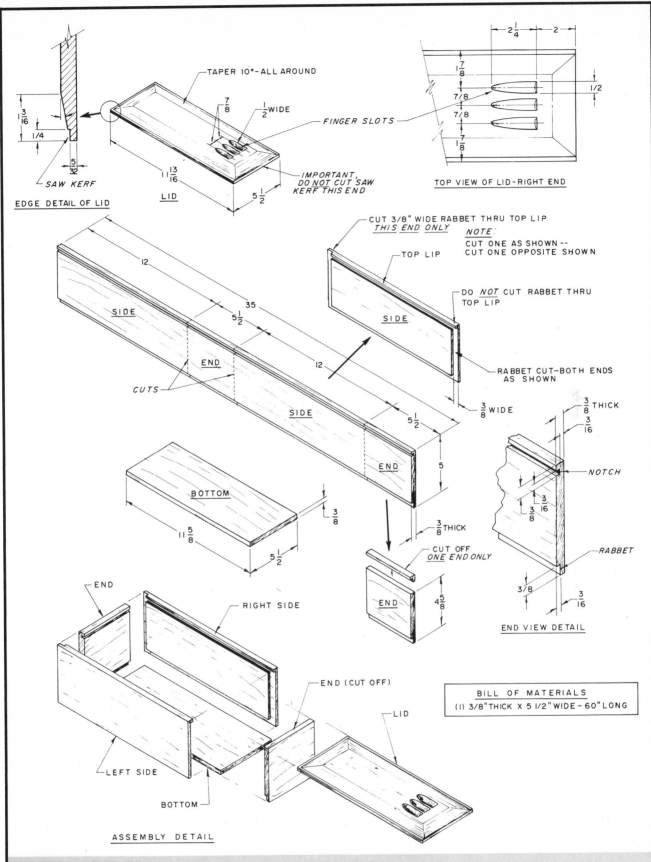

TAPER 10°-ALL AROUND

FINGER SLOTS

$\frac{7}{8}$ $\frac{1}{2}$ WIDE

TOP VIEW OF LID-RIGHT END

$2\frac{1}{4}$ 2

$1\frac{7}{8}$

$\frac{7}{8}$

$\frac{7}{8}$

$1\frac{7}{8}$

1/2

EDGE DETAIL OF LID

$\frac{3}{16}$

1/4

$\frac{5}{32}$

SAW KERF

LID

$11\frac{13}{16}$

$5\frac{1}{2}$

IMPORTANT,
DO NOT CUT SAW
KERF THIS END

CUT 3/8" WIDE RABBET THRU TOP LIP
THIS END ONLY

NOTE:
CUT ONE AS SHOWN --
CUT ONE OPPOSITE SHOWN

TOP LIP

SIDE

DO NOT CUT RABBET THRU
TOP LIP

12

SIDE

35

$5\frac{1}{2}$

12

RABBET CUT-BOTH ENDS
AS SHOWN

END

CUTS

SIDE

$\frac{3}{8}$ WIDE

$\frac{3}{8}$ THICK

$\frac{3}{16}$

$5\frac{1}{2}$

5

NOTCH

END

$\frac{3}{16}$

$\frac{3}{8}$

BOTTOM

$\frac{3}{8}$

$11\frac{5}{8}$

$5\frac{1}{2}$

$\frac{3}{8}$ THICK

RABBET

$\frac{3}{8}$

$\frac{3}{16}$

CUT OFF
ONE END ONLY

END

$4\frac{5}{8}$

END VIEW DETAIL

END

RIGHT SIDE

END (CUT OFF)

LID

LEFT SIDE

BOTTOM

ASSEMBLY DETAIL

BILL OF MATERIALS
(1) $\frac{3}{8}$"THICK X 5 1/2"WIDE - 60"LONG

Material:
Maple or any other hardwood 3/8" x 60" long (or to suit)
Sandpaper, glue, small square-cut nails
Water putty
Stain or paint

Suppliers:
Paint: Stulb Paint and Chemical Co. Inc. P.O.Box 297, Norristown, PA 19404.
Square-cut nails: Tremont Nail Co. 21 Elm St. P.O. Box 111, Wareham, MA 02571

ABOUT THE AUTHOR:
John A. Nelson is an author-woodworker from Peterborough, New Hampshire

Pipe Box

by John A. Nelson

This pipe box was found in a museum in Massachusetts and is estimted to be dated at about 1750.

In years past, when men gathered around the open fire to share one anothers company, the clay pipe was usually brought out and lit. Even in those days, smoking was thought to be dangerous. King James I stated, *"A custome lothsome to the eye, hatefull to the nose, harmefull to the braine, daungerous to the lungs, and in the blacke stinking fume thereof, neerest resembling the horrible Stigian smoke of the pit that is bottomelesse."* In spite of his warnings, tobacco addiction came to the new world anyway. Over 2,500 pounds was brought into this country in 1616, and by 1775, well over 100 million pounds. With the increased popularity of tobacco and pipe smoking, there came a need of a special place to store the longstem clay pipes of yesterday, thus the birth of the pipe box.

There probably never were two pipe boxes made alike, and they ranged from very formal, beautifully made, to rather crude boxes. These boxes were usually made of thin ¼" to 3/8" thick hard wood. Cherry, maple, mahogany or walnut was usually the wood chosen, and pine was sometimes used, especially on the more informal pipe boxes.

The open top area was where the long stemmed clay pipes were stored, and the drawer below was used to store the forbidden tobacco.

This pipe box was found in a museum in Massachusetts and is estimated to be dated at about 1750. It is somewhat unusual as it was made of pine and not as tall and thin as most pipe boxes of its day.

Today, the pipe box can still be functional for other uses and will add the warmth of yesterday to any room.

INSTRUCTIONS:

Using 3/8"thick material, cut the following parts to basic overall sizes:

- (1) Backboard — 5 3/4" wide x 16" long
- (2) Sides — 4 5/8" wide x 8 3/4" long
- (1) Frontboard — 5 3/4" wide x 5 3/4" long
- (2) Spacers — 4 1/4" wide x 6" long
- (1) Drawer front — 2 5/8" wide x 5 3/4" long

Using 1/4" thick material, cut the following parts to basic overall sizes:

- (1) Drawer back — 3" wide x 5 1/2" long
- (2) Drawer sides — 3" wide x 4" long
- (1) Drawer bottom — 3 1/2" wide x 5 1/2" long

With a light pencil, divide the top 8" of the backboard into ½" squares and transfer the shape to the wood. Carefully cut out and sand the backboard, taking care to keep the sharp edges.

With a light pencil, lay out the top design of the two sides and the front board. Carefully cut out the design and sand all over again, taking care to keep all edges sharp.

PHOTO BY DENNIS A. WATERS

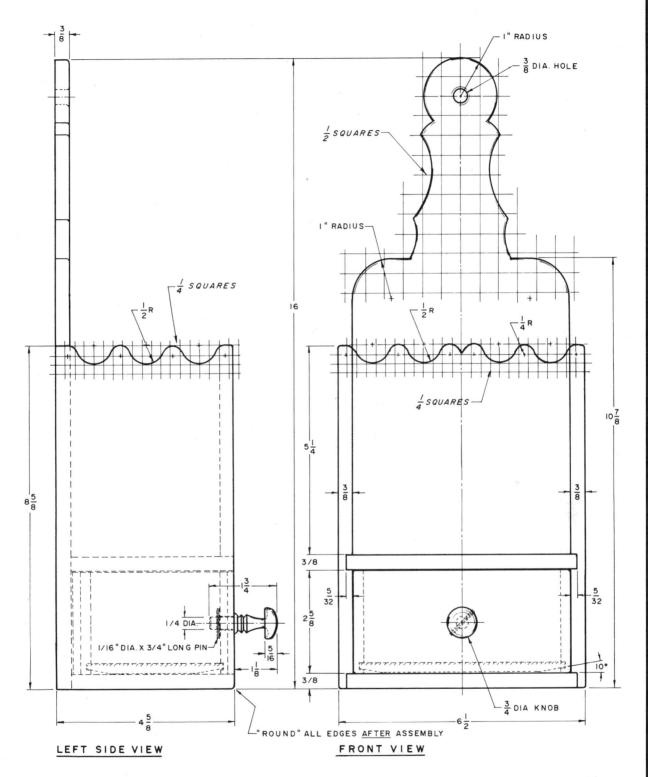

LEFT SIDE VIEW

FRONT VIEW

Drawing By The Author

today, the pipe box can still be functional for other
uses and will add the warmth of yesterday to any room.

Locate and rabbet two 3/8″ slots in the two side pieces. Make the rabbet to within 3/8″ from the back edge of the sides as shown.

Next sand the two spacers.

Dry-fit all pieces to insure correct and tight fits. Trim to fit if necessary. Lightly, glue parts together and nail with short square-cut nails. Be sure to drill small holes before nailing to avoid splitting the wood, especially near the edges.

Thoroughly sand all of the pieces. Slightly round the front edge of the top, sides and front trim designs.

Next, fit the drawer front into drawer opening. Have a snug fit at this time, rabbet for drawer bottom and sides. Rabbet the drawer back for drawer bottom, 1/8″ wide. Then rabbet the drawer sides for drawer bottom, 1/8″ wide. Bevel the four edges of the drawer bottoms at a 10 degree angle to fit into 1/8″ rabbet groove as shown. (This was done on many early made drawers and adds authenticity to your project.) Dry fit the drawer to insure correct and tight fit. Trim it to fit if necessary. Glue parts together.

Finally, fit drawer to the opening by sanding sides and bottom. Drawer should open and close with a little friction but not be sloppy.

Stain to suit. An Ipswitch Pine stain is somewhat close to the original pipe box. If you wish to make your pipe box look aged, apply a clear sealer-coat, slightly distress the surface and apply a wash coat of 50% black paint and 50% paint thinner. Wipe on and wipe right off. Leave the black wash coat in the distress marks and scratches. Try to leave some of the wash coat in the corners. It is important to experiment on some scrap wood to get the effect you want. Use two or three coats of top coat or tung oil to get a non-glossy finish. If your finish is too shiny, use #0000 steel wool to dull the finish. Apply a coat of lemon oil.

Don't forget, a new looking antique does not look right. A copy of an antique should look old, so do try the distress and wash coat effect.

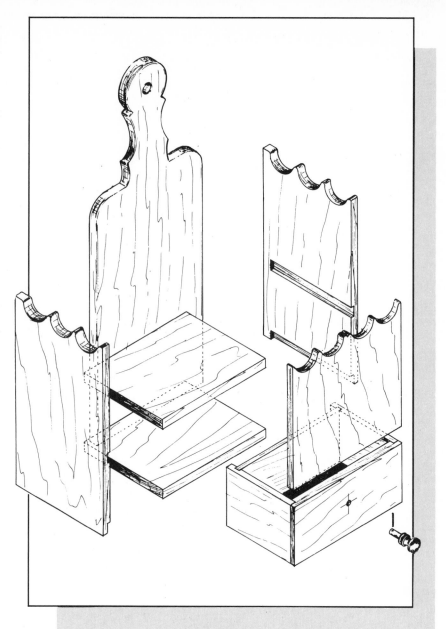

SUPPLIERS:

Paint: Stulb Paint and Chemical Co. Inc. P.O. Box 297, Norristown, PA 19404.

Square-cut nails: Tremont Nail Co., 21 Elm St., P.O. Box 111, Wareham, MA 02571.

MATERIAL:
Pine
3/8″ x 8″ — 60″ long (box)
1/4″ x 6″ — 15″ long (drawer)
Sandpaper, glue, small square cut nails
Water putty
Stain and non-glare finish coat of your choice
(tung oil recommended)

ABOUT THE AUTHOR:
John A. Nelson is an author-woodworker from Peterborough, New Hampshire.

Wall Hanging Cupboard

by John A. Nelson

If you like very early primitive antiques, this hanging wall cupboard may be for you. Although very primitive, it makes an interesting project to build, own and use.

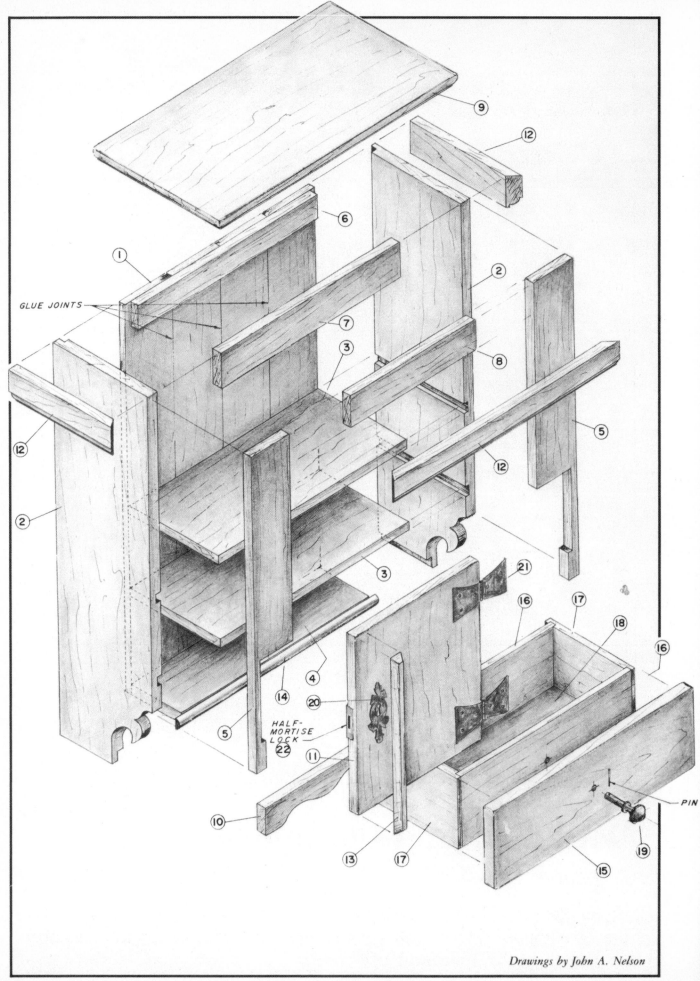

GLUE JOINTS

HALF-MORTISE LOCK

PIN

Drawings by John A. Nelson

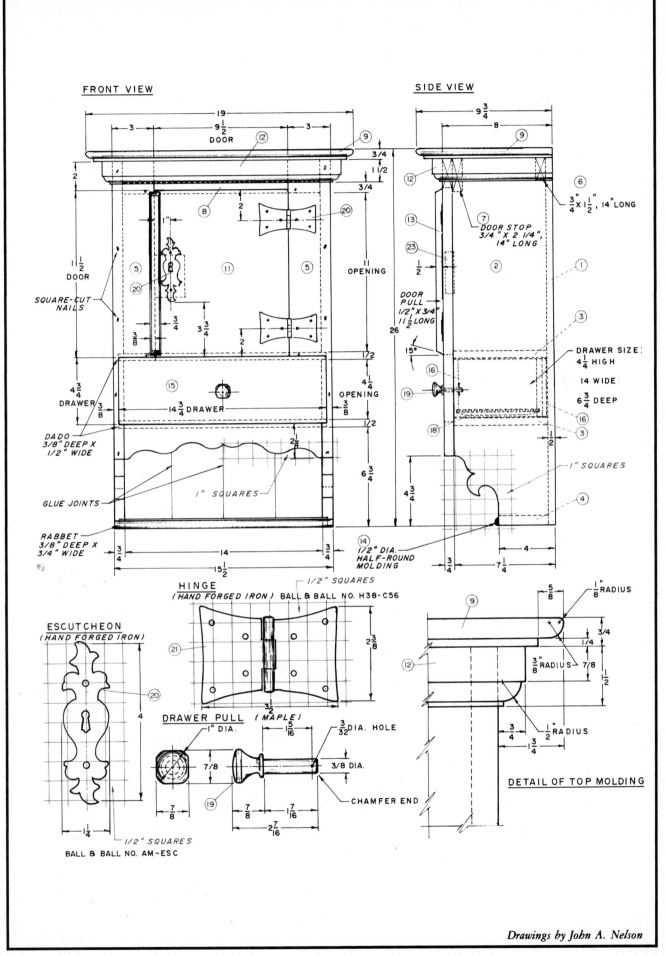

FRONT VIEW

SIDE VIEW

ESCUTCHEON
(HAND FORGED IRON)

HINGE
(HAND FORGED IRON) BALL & BALL NO. H38-C56

1/2" SQUARES

DRAWER PULL (MAPLE)

DETAIL OF TOP MOLDING

1/2" SQUARES
BALL & BALL NO. AM-ESC

Drawings by John A. Nelson

The original was found in Lancaster, Pennsylvania and was supposed to have been made around 1725; a very early piece indeed. At first glance you will say the iron butterfly hinges and escutcheon plate are much too large for such a small cupboard. I agree, but, these are the sizes that were used on the original. Mr. W. Whitman Ball of BALL AND BALL assured me that they did use very large butterfly hinges back in those days. In fact, these exact butterfly hinges and escutcheon plate are still being made and are available today.

The original cupboard was made of poplar wood and had a painted finish. Notice large handmade square-cut nails also were used, as was on the original. In fact, I took the trouble to position the nails in the exact same locations as on the original.

For that authentic look, I would recommend that you use the following materials:

Square-cut nails from: Tremont Nail Co., 21 Elm Street, P.O. Box 111, Wareham, MA 02571.

Paint from: Stulb Paint and Chemical Co., P.O. Box 297, Norristown, PA 19404 (write or call 1-800-221-8444 for their color card).

Hardware from: Ball and Ball, 463 West Lincoln Highway, Exton, PA 19341. Hand-forged iron hinges H38-C56 / Escutcheon AM-ESC ($50.00 for the set, including shipping).

Cut all pieces of wood to size, taking care to make duplicate parts exactly the same size. Cut the material for the back board, part number 1, and glue together if necessary. While letting the glue set, draw out a 1″ grid on a sheet of paper and transfer the shape of the side panel, part number 2, per the drawing. Transfer this shape onto the two side panels and cut out making both sides exactly the same. Do the same for the skirt, part number 10, and cut it out also. Cut the two dados into the sides, part number 2, as shown. Cut the notch for the drawer opening in the two front boards, part number 5, as shown, taking care to make both parts identical and all cuts at 90 degrees.

Assemble the sides, part number 2, shelves, part numbers 3 and 4, and the back, part number 1, with glue and square-cut nails, keeping everything square. Add the back support, part number 6, the support for the front, part number 7, the two front boards, part number 5, the trim, part number 8, and the bottom skirt, part number 10, again using glue and square-cut nails.

Make the top molding, part number 12, as illustrated, and add the top molding to the case, mitering the corners as shown. (A commercially made molding could be used if you cannot make the molding yourself.) Attach the top, part number 9, in place, centering it flush with the back. Add the half round molding, part number 14.

Fit the door, part number 11, to the opening and add the door pull, part number 13, to the door. Take care to overlap the door pull ⅜″ over from the edge of the door as shown. This overlap acts as a dust stop. Add the iron hinges and the escutcheon plate by first locating and drilling holes slightly smaller than the nails and nail in place. The nails that come with the hinges and escutcheon are made of soft iron and should be cleated or bent over back into the wood in the back of the door and front panel for authenticity. This is not the neatest way to do it, but it is how it was originally

done. Be sure to obtain a half mortise door lock, part number 22, with a full 1″ distance from the door edge to the keyhole to allow room for the door pull and escutcheon. This completes the case assembly.

Assemble the drawer per the drawing just slightly smaller than the drawer opening. Do not glue the drawer bottom, part number 18. Take care to keep the assembly square. The knob, part number 19, is made by first turning it to a full 1″ diameter and then sanding the four sides to the approximate ⅞″ square shape as shown. Be sure to leave the shank 1⁷⁄₁₆″ or longer in order to extend it into and through the drawer front. Pin the knob in place with either a small square-cut nail or a small wooden peg. This completes the drawer assembly.

FINISHING

This project can be either finished with a stain and a coat of tung oil or similar finish, or painted, as the original was. I tried to make my copy look very old—very close to the original—by first distressing it, then painting it off-white. I then repainted it with a coat of cabinetmaker's blue. After the paint has thoroughly dried, I carefully sanded through the blue coat here and there to simulate years of use. See the photograph. It really does look old but it is a handy cupboard and "conversational piece."

ORIGINAL MADE OF BUTTERNUT WOOD AND PAINTED

\- MATERIAL LIST \-			
NO.	NAME	SIZE	REQ'D.
1	BACK BOARD	1/2 X 14 3/4 - 25 1/4 LONG	1
2	SIDE PANEL	3/4 X 7 1/4 - 25 1/4 LONG	2
3	SHELF	1/2 X 7 1/4 - 14 3/4 LONG	2
4	BOTTOM SHELF	1/2 X 3 1/2 - 14 3/4 LONG	1
5	FRONT BOARD	3/4 X 3 - 20 1/2 LONG	2
6	BACK SUPPORT	3/4 X 1 1/2 - 14 LONG	1
7	FRONT SUPPORT	3/4 X 2 1/4 - 14 LONG	1
8	TRIM	3/4 X 2 - 9 1/2 LONG	1
9	TOP BOARD	3/4 X 9 3/4 - 19 LONG	1
10	BOTTOM SKIRT	3/4 X 2 1/4 - 14 3/4 LONG	1
11	DOOR	3/4 X 9 1/2 - 11 1/2 LONG	1
12	TOP MOLDING	3/4 X 1 1/2 - 40 LONG	1
13	DOOR PULL	1/2 X 3/4 - 11 1/2 LONG	1
14	BOTTOM MOLDING	1/2″ DIA. (1/2 ROUND)15 1/2 LG.	1
15	DRAWER FACE	3/4 X 4 3/4 - 14 3/4 LONG	1
16	DRAWER FRONT/BACK	1/2 X 4 1/4 - 13 1/2 LONG	1
17	DRAWER SIDE	1/2 X 4 1/4 - 6 3/4 LONG	2
18	DRAWER BOTTOM	3/8 X 6 1/4 - 13 1/2 LONG	1
19	DRAWER PULL	1″ DIA. - 2 7/16 LONG	1
20	ESCUTCHEON	B & B NUMBER AM-ESC	1
21	HINGE-BUTTERFLY	B & B NUMBER H38-C56	2
22	HALF-MORTISE LOCK	1″ FROM SIDE TO KEYHOLE	1
\-	SQUARE-CUT NAIL	1 1/2″ LONG	30

PART NOS. 16, 17 & 18 MADE FROM PINE

ABOUT THE AUTHOR:

*John A. Nelson is a contributing editor of **The American Woodworker**.*

When initially conceiving an idea for a new wood item, one ultimately tries to think of a shape that can uniquely display wood's inherent beauty. At the same time, it's nice to come up with a design that has some function and perhaps even something that can be handled or felt. The pens certainly seem to serve these prerequisites.

Desk Pen & Pencil Set

by Jeff Armstrong

Photo by the author

I was taught to make writing instruments of wood by a true artist and craftsman, Michael Bailot. He is one of those gifted people who constantly is bombarded by an almost overpowering flow of creativity. Often it seems his only limitation is the time it takes to master a new craft.

For me, making these writing instruments was a most refreshing experience. Turning was a whole new challenge and the material itself was very different from the domestic hardwoods I was so used to ripping, crosscutting, shaping and sanding. All the pens and pencils are made from tropical hardwoods. We make the desk sets out of five of these beautiful woods: cordia from Mexico, cardinal wood from Brazil, morado from Bolivia, cocobolo from parts of Central America and tulipwood from Africa. The directions following are an invitation to discover delicate wood turning and a whole new world of materials.

To begin, rip several pieces of the wood of your choice ½" square, then crosscut at perfect 90 degree angles 8½" long. Be sure to make some extra pieces to practice on. Next, round the ends on a belt sander for 1" of length on only one end. These ends need not be perfectly round, just able to insert into a ½" three jaw chuck.

For the first lathe step, the stock needs to be drilled for the metal bushing the pen tip fits into and for the refill or the pencil mechanism. The processes are the same for the pen and pencil and the hardware is interchangeable. Mark the center of the square end with a nail, then insert the rounded end in the three jaw chuck in the headstock. Snug the jaws firmly by hand. Next, insert a #9 aircraft drill in the three jaw chuck in the tailstock. Adjust the tailstock so the drill is only a fraction of an inch from the end of the pen blank. Turn the pen blank by hand while extending the drill a little at a time with the screw crank for about ½" for a pilot hole. Leaving the drill inside the hole, turn on the lathe at a low rpm. After loosening the tailstock, drill a hole 4" deep by actually moving the complete tailstock drill assembly, as a unit, in and out of the wood. Note: due to the resin content of most tropical hardwoods, the drill will have to be removed and cleaned fairly often for a hole this deep.

Prepare for turning by supergluing the threaded bushing ⅛" from the hole end of the stock, then screw in the pen tip. If a pencil is being made, skip this step and just push the threaded bushing in the tip for a friction fit. Insert a live ball bearing center in the tailstock and snug it up to the pen tip. With a ½" gouge turn the blank round not less than ⅜" diameter, occasionally checking the chuck and center for snugness. Make pencil marks for the end of the pen (about 7") and for any detail work you care to do. Shape the barrel down to the metal tip at least 1⁄64" oversize to allow for sanding. We use a ¼" skew for most ornamental turning like balls and grooves. It's best when cutting to begin at a point farthest from the headstock and work in. This procedure helps eliminate breakage. Imagination is the only limitation at this point! To make the more streamlined version, the gouge will do all of the shaping and the skew will cut the three grooves.

Begin sanding with the finest grit possible to remove tool marks and work up to 220#. Steel wool with 0000 while the pen is rotating, then with the lathe off, sand and steel wool with the grain. The extra pen tip is for the finished pen; the other for turning and sanding just in case it's scratched. Use the parting tool or skew to separate the pen from the chucked end. With practice the pen can be parted off into the free hand. Finally, touch up the top end with a piece of sandpaper and steel wool. If the more streamlined version is being made, bevel the end and then touch up with sandpaper.

Finish with linseed oil or another oil of your choice. The hole length in the procedure above is for a Cross type refill. Before inserting the refill use a very small piece of foam to cushion writing. Minute adjustments can be made in hole length by carefully sanding the front of the barrel if the refill is loose.

For the pen and pencil base, begin setups with a matching or contrasting wood. Plane the 4/4 or 5/4 material 7/8". Keep in mind when purchasing the material that quite often 4/4 rough lumber can be up to 1¼" in thickness. Rip 2¾" then crosscut 7". For a sleek profile set up the table saw for a 20 degree bevel and cut all four sides top and bottom to leave an edge thickness of ⅜". To drill the pen and pencil holes in the base a jig needs to be made to hold the base at a 20 degree angle to the drill bit. Next grind a 5/16" twist drill to the same taper as the pen or pencil tip excluding the refill. Mark the hole locations 1" from the top edge and 1½" from each side. Before drilling that valuble piece of exotic hardwood it's best to check the following setup with a piece of scrap. Drill the two holes 9/16" deep with the angle fixture. Next drill two more holes 3/32" for the refill. A good idea is to drill both holes the same so the pen or pencil can fit in either hole. Check for fit and adjust as needed.

Belt sand, finish sand and steel wool to a satin finish. Use the same oil as the writing instruments. A piece of adhesive felt cut to size on the bottom adds that professional touch.

To make the round base, begin by cutting a 1⅛" to 1¼" thick piece of wood to match the pen 3¼" in diameter with a hole saw or band saw. Drill a ¼" hole in the center and mount on the lathe with a screw chuck. With the gouge,

turn the base to a pleasing contour top and bottom. If an alternative method is used to mount the base stock to the lathe, the ¼" hole may be unnecessary. Sand and steel wool on the lathe. Plug the hole with a ¼" dowel if the screw chuck was used and, with the jig above, drill the stepped hole for the pen. For a more finished look the pen tip hole can be drilled a little deeper and the top can be countersunk. Finish as above with the oil of choice and add a piece of felt for the bottom.

Refills, threaded bushings, pen tips and pencil mechanisms can be ordered from Expressly Wood, Rt. 2, Box 492, Huntsville, AR 72740.

Bill of Material

The dimensions below are for planed or ripped material.

DESCRIPTION	QUANTITY	T	W	L
Pen and Pencil Stock	several pieces	½"	½"	8½"
Pen and Pencil Base	one	⅞"	2¾"	7"
Pen Base	one	1⅛"	3½"	3½"
Felt for Large Base	one		1½"	5½"
Felt for Small Base	one	2½" round		
Pencil Mechanism 11 mm	one			
Pen Tip	two per pen			
Threaded Bushing	one per pen			
Cross type ball point refill	one			

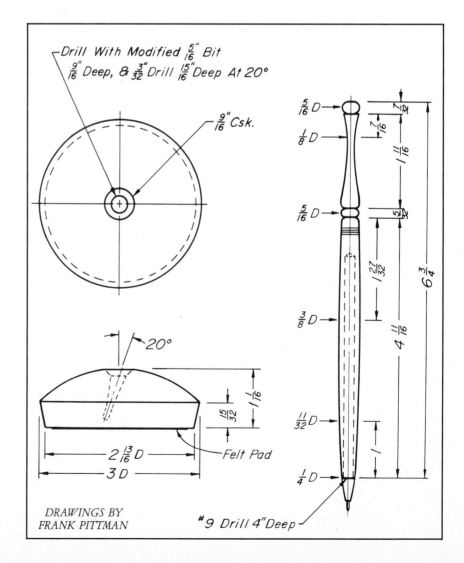

Drill With Modified 5/16" Bit 9/16" Deep, & 3/32 Drill 15/16" Deep At 20°

9/16" Csk.

5/16 D
⅛ D
5/16 D
3/8 D
11/32 D
¼ D

7/32
7/16
11/16
5/32
1 27/32
4 11/16
6 ¾
1

20°
15/32
1/16
2 13/16 D
3 D
Felt Pad

#9 Drill 4" Deep

DRAWINGS BY FRANK PITTMAN

32

*Do you have books stacked up
in out of the way places, unorganized and hard to get to?
Maybe one of these bookracks can help.*

BOOKRACKS
by Jeff Armstrong

PHOTOGRAPH BY THE AUTHOR

These racks are great for keeping those frequently used cookbooks handy on the counter or for keeping dictionaries and reference books within arms' reach on the desk. Even video tapes can be lined up in one of these bookracks.

We make three different styles of racks. One we laminate at random with many different hardwoods, one is walnut with thin padauk and oak stripes, and one is oak with thin padauk and walnut stripes. All the bookracks use three ½" dowels for the adjustable support to slide upon. The bookracks can be made from most species of wood and dowels may be shorter or longer, depending on individual needs.

To begin, plane 1" or 1¼" thick oak, padauk and walnut to 7/8". The oak we get from the mills here in Arkansas is usually oversize so we have plenty of room for the 7/8" pieces from 1" stock. Crosscut to 19½" then rip into strips of 1¼". Six strips of the oak and one strip each of the padauk and walnut are used for each bookrack.

Rip or resaw the walnut and padauk. Then plane or flat sand to 3/16" to finish up with one strip each of 3/16" thick, 1¼" wide and 19½" long. Next, lay out five strips of oak, one thin walnut, one thin padauk and one oak. If a planer will be used to smooth the faces after laminating, it's best to orient the grain in each strip the same in order to reduce tearout. Glue and clamp, taking care that all joints stay even with each other. Since padauk is a resinous wood, wash it with lacquer thinner or a mix of vinegar and water before gluing.

When the lamination is dry, plane very carefully or sand with a wide belt to 1". Crosscut first to square the edge, then cut two 6¾" pieces and one 2 7/8" piece. Sand end grain with 120 grit on all three pieces.

Drill the three dowel holes in both end pieces. Since dowels are not produced exactly to ½" in all cases, a 33/64" bit may work better. Check the dowels with a hole drilled in a piece of scrap first. The holes are drilled ½" deep in both end pieces. Refer to the drawing for the hole locations.

The holes in the center piece are 9/16" in diameter and are drilled completely through.

Rout perimeters on all four sides, top and bottom, of all three pieces with a ¼" or 3/8" round over bit. Drum sand to 150 grit, rounding over the edges and blending them into the faces inside and outside. Crosscut a ½" dowel to 18" and assemble the 6¾" end to the 2 7/8" end with the 6¾" sliding piece in between.

Use the finish of your choice and the bookrack is ready for service.

ABOUT THE AUTHOR:

Jeff Armstrong is a contributing editor to **The American Woodworker.**

BILL OF MATERIAL

Code	Part	Quantity	T × W × L
A	End	1	1 × 5½ × 6¾
B	Slider	1	1 × 5½ × 6¾
C	End	1	1 × 5½ × 2 7/8
D	Dowels	3	½" dia. × 18"

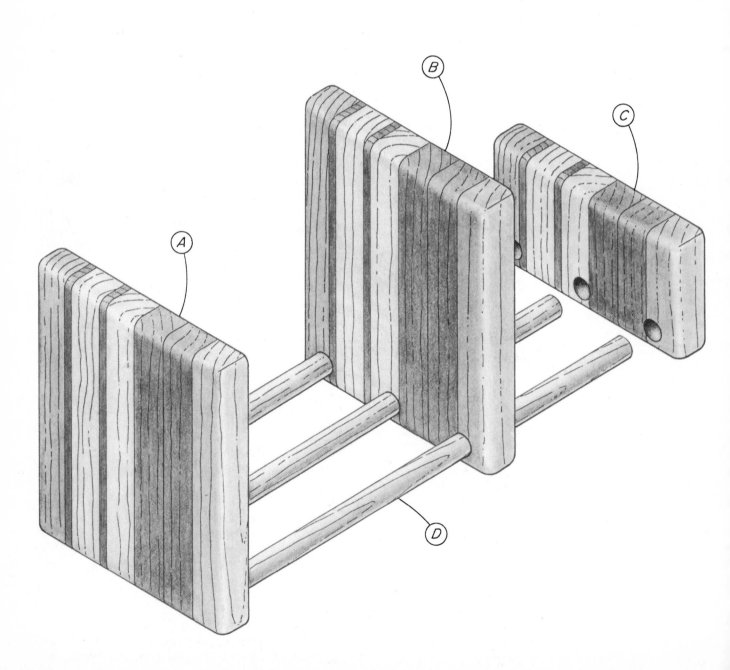

Picture Frames

Some Tools and Methods To Make The Job Easier

By Dennis R. Watson

Picture frames are some of the easiest and quickest projects you can make if you have the right equipment and use the correct methods. This article actually describes two projects. The first shows how to construct a simple jig that can be used to cut the groove for a spline used in the picture frame. It can also be used to cut other joints. The second project details some different methods used in producing picture frames. We will begin with the jig.

Tenoning Jig/Frame Board

The tenoning/spline jig is a simple homemade jig which holds a board vertical while the board/jig is moved along the rip fence through the blade. The jig and a sharp blade will cut a clean, true groove for a spline, the cheek of a tenon or open mortise. A groove for a corner spline can be cut through a 45 degree miter joint with the addition of the frame board which holds the frame at a 45 degree angle to the table saw.

Cut two pieces of ¾ inch plywood, one 4¾ inches wide, the other 5½ inches wide and glue them together for the base. The difference in width forms a rabbet for the vertical piece which is glued and screwed to the base. Clamp the two braces in place and check to see if the vertical piece is square to the table, then glue and screw them in place. I added a couple of hardwood blocks, the front one is a hand hold and the rear one provides a clamping surface. Screw the ¾ x ¾ inch back-up board in place, don't glue as you'll want to replace it as necessary. The back-up board supports the board and also reduces tear out.

The frame board is a piece of ¾ inch plywood with two removable support blocks. The blocks which are rotated 45 degrees to the table not only hold the frame in position but they also support the back side of the cut reducing tear out. The blocks are screwed in a ¾ inch groove, which makes replacing them easy since realignment is not necessary. Be sure to place the lower screw about three inches above the bottom of the board which assures you of not hitting the screw with the saw blade. When screwing the frame board to the tenoning/spline jig check the alignment with a 45 degree square.

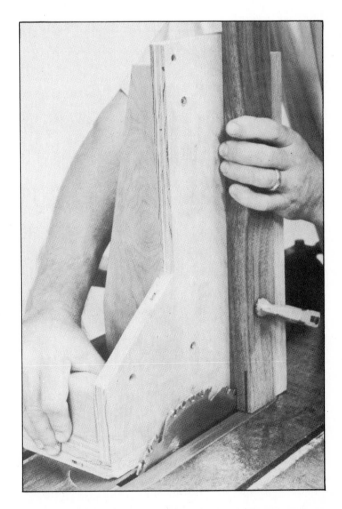

A tenon or groove is cut in the end of a board using the tenoning jig. The board is clamped to the jig and slid along the rip fence past the blade.

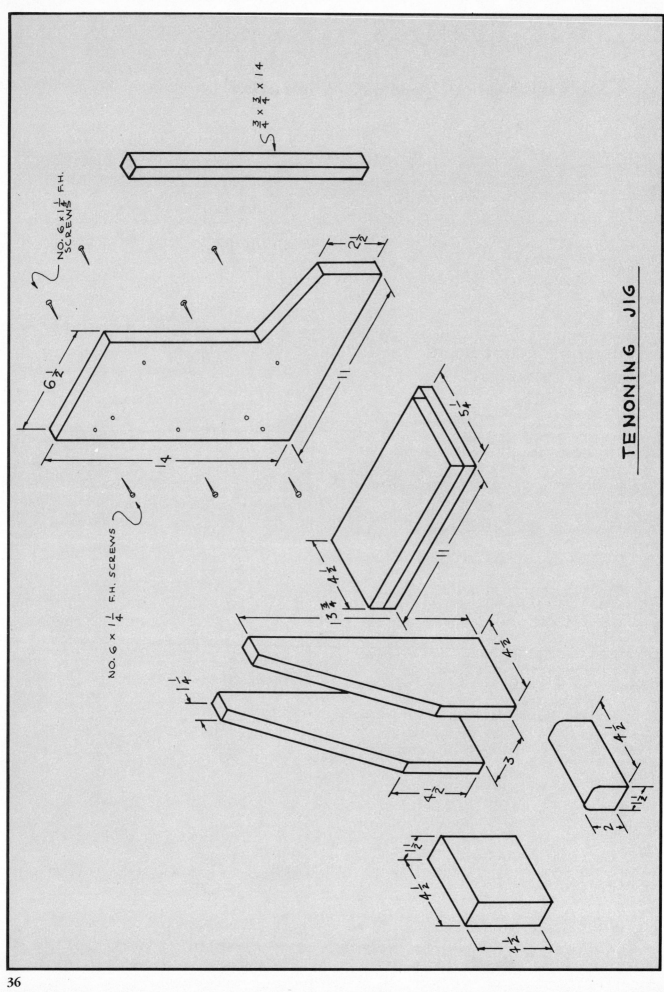

$\frac{3}{4} \times \frac{3}{4} \times 14$

NO. 6 × 1$\frac{1}{4}$ F.H. SCREWS

NO. 6 × 1$\frac{1}{4}$ F.H. SCREWS

2$\frac{1}{2}$

6$\frac{1}{2}$

14

11

5$\frac{1}{4}$

11

4$\frac{1}{2}$

13$\frac{3}{4}$

4$\frac{1}{2}$

1$\frac{1}{4}$

3

4$\frac{1}{2}$

4$\frac{1}{2}$

1$\frac{1}{2}$

2

4$\frac{1}{2}$

4$\frac{1}{2}$

1$\frac{1}{2}$

TENONING JIG

When the frame board is screwed to the tenoning jig, corner joints can be grooved to accept a spline for additional strength.

The vertical piece is reinforced with two stiffners. The front hardwood block is a handhold and the rear one provides a clamping surface.

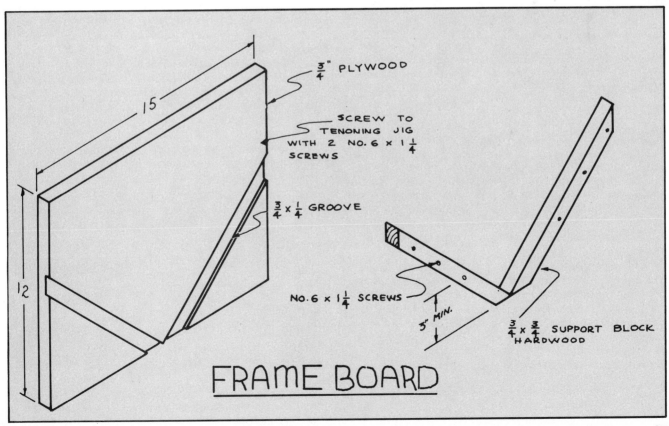

$\frac{3}{4}$" PLYWOOD

15

SCREW TO TENONING JIG WITH 2 NO. 6 x 1$\frac{1}{4}$ SCREWS

$\frac{3}{4}$ x $\frac{1}{4}$ GROOVE

12

NO. 6 x 1$\frac{1}{4}$ SCREWS

5" MIN.

$\frac{3}{4}$ x $\frac{3}{4}$ SUPPORT BLOCK HARDWOOD

FRAME BOARD

Picture Frames

The family portraits of that picture of grandmother found hiding away in the attic surely deserves a beautiful wood frame. However, quality wood frames 5''x7'', 8''x10'', etc. can be quite expensive. This was the incentive for me to dig through my scrap wood pile for suitable wood to make several frames. The frames are designed to hang on a wall or sit on a desk. A small arm folds out from the back to support the frame when it is sitting upright.

After the design is selected and the molding cut, there are two basic operations to consider when making frames. The first is mitering the corners; the second is clamping the joints. Clamping can be avoided altogether - a small step for mankind but a giant step for the framemaker. The joints are glued and simply rubbed together. This does not produce a strong joint until a 1/8 inch slot is cut across the joint and a spline glued in place. This makes the joint extremely strong. In addition, the color contrast of the spline, which can be increased by using different woods, adds to the visual interest of the frame.

Select the stock and shape it to the desired profile.

Moulding for the frames was made on a shaper. Note the use of a push stick and a feather board to safely shape a small strip of wood.

The profile is cut in a variety of ways, a moulding head on the radial arm or table saw, a router mounted upside down in a router table or a shaper. The shape of the moulding depends mostly on the cutters available. Cutters, of course can be combined to form many different shapes. After the moulding has been cut, run a ¼ inch deep slot about ¼ inch wide on the back side. The width is not critical. Then run a ½ inch deep slot slightly wider than the backing material - 3/16 inch for the frames shown. The spacing of this slot is critical; it should provide a rabbet for the glass plus the picture to sit in.

The next step is to miter the ends to the desired length. The miters can be cut in a variety of ways; a table saw, radial arm saw or by hand using a miter box. In any case they must be cut precisely; the smallest error when multiplied by four will show up as a gap. I found the best way to get a true 45 degree miter is to make the cut in two scrap pieces of wood, put the joint together and check the angle with a square. If the frame is perfectly square you then have a perfect 45 degree miter.

The frames are easily assembled by simply placing a small amount of yellow glue on each end and rubbing the joint together; when the glue becomes tacky and resists the

movement, set the two pieces aside to dry. After the glue has dried (about an hour) the two half frames can be assembled in a similar manner. Sometimes, if the moulding is slightly bowed it may be necessary to use clamps. However, clamping is much easier since two of the joints are already glued. These joints are not extremely strong but their main purpose is to hold the frame together until the slot is cut for the splines.

Splines were made from matching wood and glued in place; be sure to clamp the splines using a ''C'' clamp and some scrap blocks of wood. After the glue has dried trim the splines with a sharp chisel. The splines can be made from contrasting wood to add an interesting visual touch to the frame. Readily available model airplane plywood, 3/32 or 1/8 inch, also makes an interesting spline.

If the frames are going to sit on a desk or table a back with a swing out support arm will have to be made. The frames shown have a 3/16 inch plywood back but ¼ inch plywood or masonite will work fine. Cut the 1½ x 5 inch slot in the back and rip a strip to fit inside the slot. Select a hinge which is fairly large then route a recess in the back side of the plywood the size and shape of the hinge. Drill a few extra holes in the hinge to increase the effectiveness of the glue, then glue the hinge in place using epoxy glue. Once the glue has dried open the support; it probably will not open far enough and you'll have

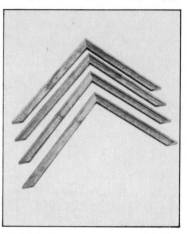

The miter joints are simply rubbed together and set aside to dry.

to bevel the end of the support arm with a chisel until the arm opens up about two inches.

If you are not going to sit the frame on a desk or table, the swing out arm is not needed. The backing material can be almost anything; heavy cardboard, foam board, 1/8 inch masonite, etc.

When hanging a frame I prefer to use two attach points which keeps the frame from tilting. Two holes can be drilled in the frame or a special picture frame router bit is available which cuts a keyhole-shaped hole in the back of the frame. The bit is run straight into the frame then pushed toward the top of the frame producing a lip which grips a large headed nail. To hang the frame it is placed over a large headed nail then moved down. If you plan on making many frames the router bit is nice to have.

Slots for the 1/8 inch spline are cut across the miter joint. A homemade jig is used to hold the frame vertically, frame and jig are slid past blade.

Splines are glued in the slots cut through the corners of the frame to strengthen the miter joints.

Apply your favorite finish, then cut the glass to complete the project. For a first rate job non-glare glass can be used or non-breakable plexiglass can be used for a childs room.

The interior side of the back is mortised to accept the hinge. Additional holes are drilled in the hinge to increase effectiveness of the epoxy glue.

A router is used to remove wood from one end of the frame which allows the back to slide in.

A small support arm folds out to support the frame when it sits on a desk or table.

ABOUT THE AUTHOR
Dennis R. Watson makes his living as an Aerospace Engineer. He enjoys making his own furniture. He is a frequent contributor to various magazines.

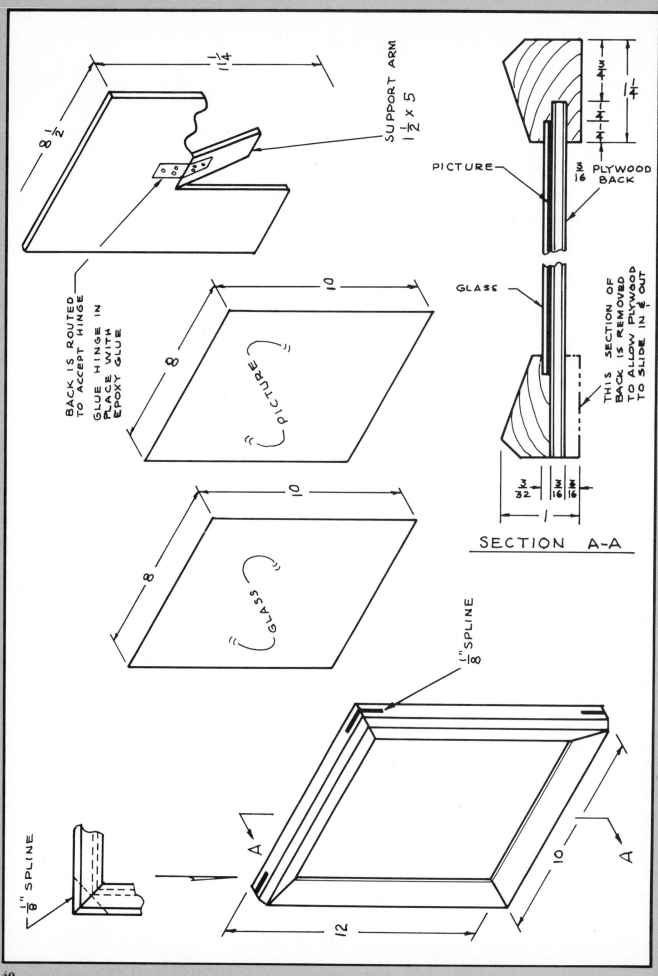

SUPPORT ARM
1½ × 5

11¼

8½

BACK IS ROUTED
TO ACCEPT HINGE

GLUE HINGE IN
PLACE WITH
EPOXY GLUE

10

8

(PICTURE

10

8

(GLASS

PICTURE

GLASS

¾
16 PLYWOOD
BACK

THIS SECTION OF
BACK IS REMOVED
TO ALLOW PLYWOOD
TO SLIDE IN & OUT

¾
4

¼
4

¼
4

1¼

3
32

3
16

3
16

1

SECTION   A-A

⅛" SPLINE

⅛" SPLINE

A

A

12

10

40

Wastebasket

By Carlyle Lynch

As every woodworker knows, scraps tend to accumulate in a shop. Sometimes they represent a fair amount of money and deserve to be used. After one project, I had left over strips of 1/4 inch white pine plywood that I used to make this wastebasket.

"The lace also acts as a stop for your fingers when picking up the basket…"

The drawing and material bill shows that sixteen strips of plywood are nailed to a square base with nails whose heads can be hidden by driving brass ornamental furniture nails over them. Holes drilled as shown allow a rawhide boot lace to hold the pieces together at the top in an attractive pattern. The lacing also acts as a stop for your fingers when picking up the basket to empty it.

Use a fine tooth (plywood) saw blade to cut the strips. Drill the holes in them while the strips are clamped to a piece of scrap to prevent splintering. Carefully sand all arises to soften the edges. Sand the face sides to remove any mill marks and finish all pieces before assembly.

Carlyle Lynch is a retired teacher living in Broadway, VA.

WASTEBASKET

$\frac{3}{8}$

$\frac{3}{16}$ Drill

Rawhide lacing, smooth side out.

$\frac{1}{2}$

Face side corners well sanded

1 in.

Scale

Construction at corners.

$14\frac{1}{2}$

$\frac{1}{4}$ Ply.

9

$2\frac{1}{4}$ $2\frac{1}{4}$

No. 9 Polished or antiqued brass furniture nail.

$\frac{3}{4}$

45°

$\frac{1}{4}$

2d. Fin. nail under ornamental brass nail.

Materials:
8 pcs. ply. $\frac{1}{4}$ x $2\frac{1}{4}$ x $14\frac{1}{4}$ corners
8 "   " $\frac{1}{4}$ x $2\frac{1}{4}$ x $13\frac{1}{4}$ centers
1 "   " $\frac{1}{4}$ x $8\frac{1}{2}$ x $8\frac{1}{2}$ bottom

32 2d. finishing nails
32 No. 9 brass furniture nails
8' (apprx) Rawhide boot lacing.

E.C. LYNCH

Telephone Center

by John A. Nelson

Have you ever picked up the phone and had an important message to write down only to find you didn't have a pencil, or a piece of paper within reaching distance? Well, hopefully, this weekend project will solve that problem for you. Not only does this telephone center provide a convenient place to store pencils and paper, it also dresses up a wall phone so it will blend into the room decor.

This project can be made of most any kind of wood and can be stained or painted, as this example has been. I chose paint for my project to coordinate with the color scheme of the room the telephone is in.

As with any project, even simple ones such as this, it is a good idea to study the plans so you know exactly how the project is constructed.

Carefully draw out a ½″ grid in a piece of cardboard or, if you intend to make several phone centers, use a piece of thin plywood for a full size pattern. Transfer the shape, square-for-square as illustrated on the plans. As this is somewhat a simple shape, this should not be very difficult.

Cut all ½″ thick wood to the exact given sizes on the bill of materials. Keep everything square as you proceed. Where duplicate sizes are required, cut all parts with a saw stop-set at the exact size so the parts will match.

Transfer the patterns to the wood that has been cut to overall size. The only difficult part of this project is cutting out the shape of parts (1) side, (2) backboard, and (3) platform. If you have a band saw, jig saw or a sabre saw this really is not very hard. After these parts have been cut out, sand all edges, keeping all edges sharp.

Note: simple butt joints have been used throughout this project. If you are an advanced woodworker you might wish to dado part (1) side for top shelf, (6) bottom and (8) fence, and dado part (3) platform, but I do not think this is necessary as the phone center is very rugged. If you do dado, don't forget to add enough extra material to parts 4, 5, 6 and 8 to reach into the dados.

Sand all surfaces of all parts at this time taking care not to "round" any edges.

Dry-fit all pieces to check for good tight fits at all joints. The project is now ready for assembly.

ASSEMBLY

Glue and nail part (3) platform to part (4) front board, taking care to keep a 90 degree bend between parts. Add part (9) brace and part (7) lip to this assembly. Put aside to set.

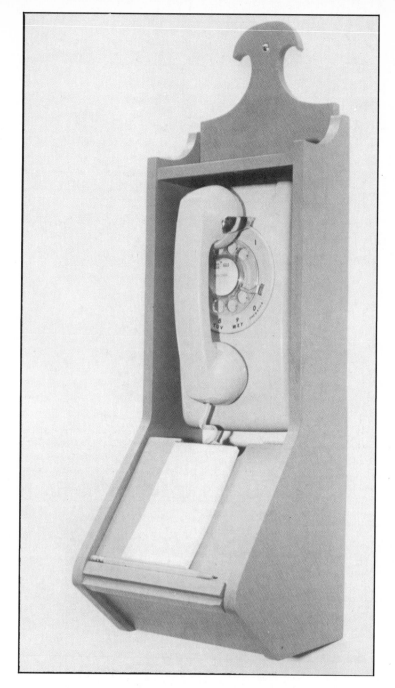

Assemble part (6) bottom with part (8) fence, again taking care to have a 90 degree bend between parts.

Assemble part (2) backboard with part (5) top shelf, keeping a 90 degree bend between parts as shown.

Carefully mark the locations on one of the interior surfaces of part (1) side using the actual parts as a pattern. Place the other (opposite) interior surface of part (1) side side-by-side to the marked up side and transfer the exact locations to this side. Take care that both sides are exactly the same and that you have marked both interior surfaces.

Assemble parts (2) and (5) to the sides, part (1) parts (6) and (8) to the sides, part (1), taking care to keep everything on your marks and square as you proceed. Allow time for the glue to set.

Locate the hole for the two screws, part (11), and drill through the sides, part (1) as shown. Take extra care that the platform assembly, parts (3), (4), (7) and (9) swing freely. Turn the assembly over, locate and glue the two stops, part (10), in place as shown. I added magnetic door catches (not shown) next to the stops in order that the platform stay securely closed.

42

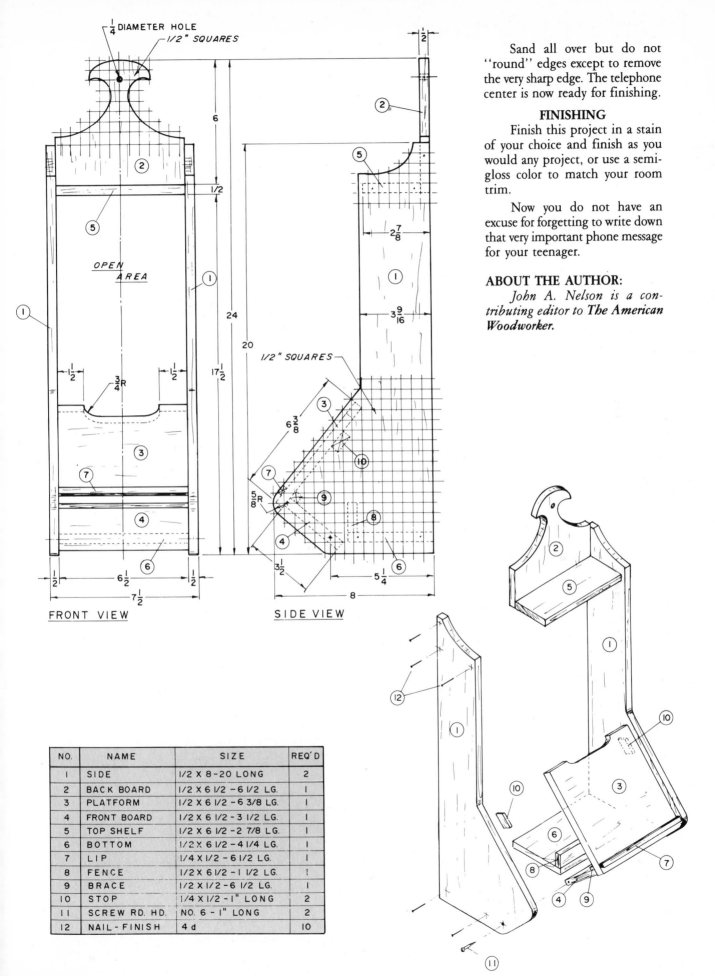

Sand all over but do not "round" edges except to remove the very sharp edge. The telephone center is now ready for finishing.

FINISHING

Finish this project in a stain of your choice and finish as you would any project, or use a semi-gloss color to match your room trim.

Now you do not have an excuse for forgetting to write down that very important phone message for your teenager.

ABOUT THE AUTHOR:

John A. Nelson is a contributing editor to **The American Woodworker.**

FRONT VIEW

SIDE VIEW

NO.	NAME	SIZE	REQ'D
1	SIDE	1/2 X 8-20 LONG	2
2	BACK BOARD	1/2 X 6 1/2 – 6 1/2 LG.	1
3	PLATFORM	1/2 X 6 1/2 – 6 3/8 LG.	1
4	FRONT BOARD	1/2 X 6 1/2 – 3 1/2 LG.	1
5	TOP SHELF	1/2 X 6 1/2 – 2 7/8 LG.	1
6	BOTTOM	1/2 X 6 1/2 – 4 1/4 LG.	1
7	LIP	1/4 X 1/2 – 6 1/2 LG.	1
8	FENCE	1/2 X 6 1/2 – 1 1/2 LG.	1
9	BRACE	1/2 X 1/2 – 6 1/2 LG.	1
10	STOP	1/4 X 1/2 – 1" LONG	2
11	SCREW RD. HD.	NO. 6 – 1" LONG	2
12	NAIL – FINISH	4 d	10

CLOTHES CADDY

by Bill Marsella

*T*his "gentlemen's valet" is not only a welcome addition to the bedroom, but a simple and useful project for the home woodworker. The unit illustrated was constructed entirely from American walnut—the only exceptions were a short length of 1/8″ diameter aluminum rod, a brass coat hook, a small piece of 1/8″ ply that was covered with felt, and a short length of vinyl "T" edge. The original stock came from an Arkansas sawmill as 4/4KD and was planed to 3/4 in my shop.

Trouser Board Fig. 1

(See Detail "A"—main drawing) This was constructed from solid walnut and after the segments were matched for figure and internal stress, they were glued and dowelled together to make the required width. The top edge was slotted with a back saw (one with a narrow kerf) to receive the vinyl "T" edge. This operation was done on the bench. The thought that this slot could easily be done on the bench saw is tempting but inadvisable. It is not only dangerous, but the thickness of a mitre blade is too wide for this slot. If you have the right fittings for the router, this method would be to your advantage.

Back Frame Fig. 2

Once the trouser board has been set into the clamps the back frame is constructed next. It is a simple frame, dowelled together at the joints, but it must be machined accurately and clamped squarely. Hand scrape and sand the inside edges of the frame before gluing to avoid the tedious job of trying to clean the corners after the frame is assembled.

Support Rods Fig. 3

Since the trouser board must be at an angle and the only support of this part is at the very bottom (as it joins the back frame), some support is needed, not only for the finished unit,

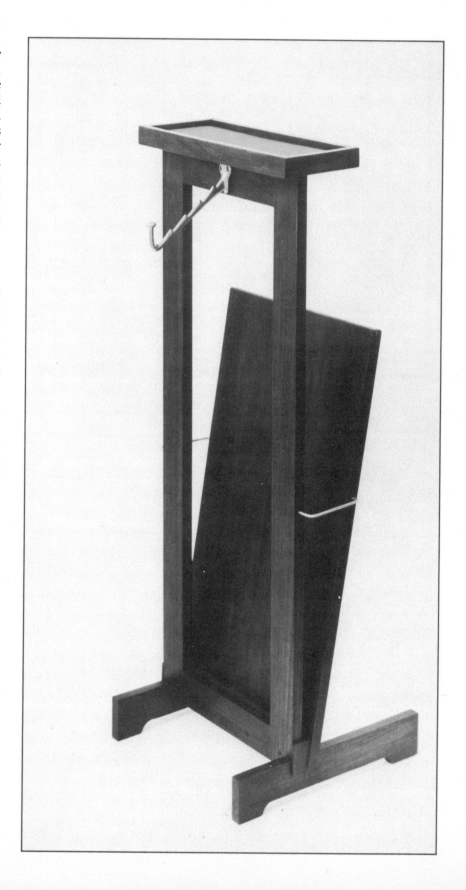

CLOTHES CADDY

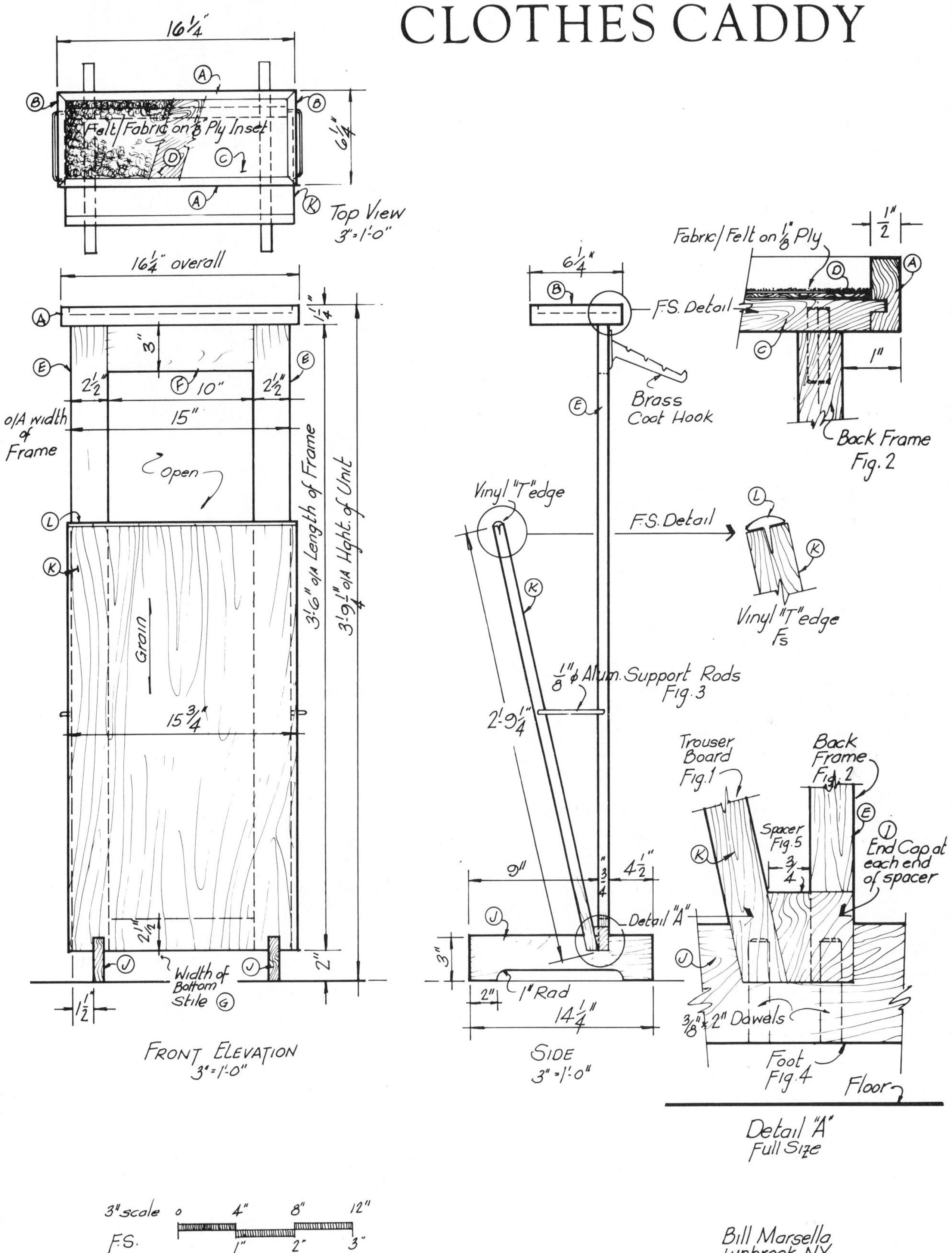

16¼"

Felt Fabric on ⅛ Ply Inset

6¼"

Top View
3" = 1'-0"

16¼" overall

3"

2½"   10   2½"

o/A width of Frame

15"

← open →

Grain

15¾"

3'-6" o/a Length of Frame

3'-9¼" o/A Hght. of Unit

2½"

1½"

2"

Width of Bottom Stile Ⓖ

FRONT ELEVATION
3" = 1'-0"

6¼"

Ⓑ

F.S. Detail

Brass Coat Hook

Ⓔ

Vinyl "T" edge

2'-9¼"

F.S. Detail →

Vinyl "T" edge
F.S.

⅛"⌀ Alum. Support Rods
Fig. 3

9"   ¾"   4½"

3"

2"   1" Rad

14¼"

SIDE
3" = 1'-0"

Detail "A"

Fabric / Felt on ⅛" Ply

½"

Ⓐ Ⓓ

Ⓒ

1"

Back Frame
Fig. 2

Trouser Board
Fig. 1

Back Frame
Fig. 2

Spacer Fig. 5

¾

End Cap at each end of spacer

⅜" x 2" Dowels

Foot
Fig. 4

Floor

Detail "A"
Full Size

3" scale   0   4"   8"   12"

F.S.   1"   2"   3"

Bill Marsella
Lynbrook, NY

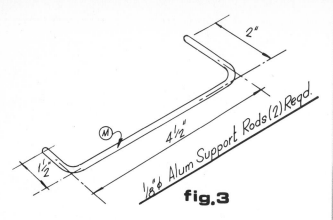

2"

4½"

1/8"∅ Alum Support Rods (2) Reqd.

1½"

Ⓜ

fig.3

but also while handling and finishing the unit; so these stays should be made now. Once the stock is cut to length, they are secured in a machinist's vise (protected from the jaws with cardboard) and bent to shape. This method will permit less of a radius at the bends than could be obtained in a wooden jig. The angles of the bends are 90º, and each of the legs must align with the centerline of the rod. If you remove the burrs from the cut ends, the rods will be easier to set into the holes of the back frame and trouser board later on.

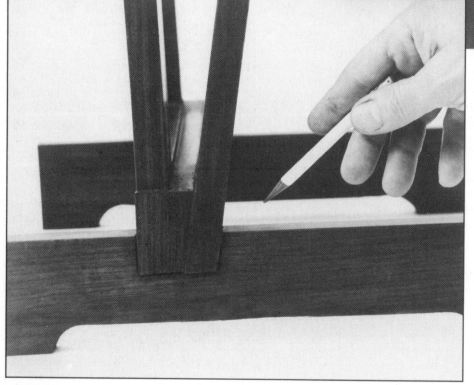

FEET...This notch must be cut to form a tight joint.

Feet Fig. 4

Two feet will be required (see drawing), and the wood for them must be selected with strength and stability in mind. They must be sound because a notch will be cut into them to receive the superstructure. This notch must be cut to form a tight joint.

Spacer Fig. 5

This is the part that will determine the angle of the trouser board. It was ripped on the bench saw from a piece of 3/4" walnut. While you have the arbor set for this cut, leave it in position, change the blade, and cross cut the bottom edge of

Locate the position of the aluminum rod stays and drill 1/8" holes, 1" deep in the outer edge of the frame and the trouser board.

the trouser board. Along with this piece, you will need two walnut end caps (Part I) which will be joined to this spacer at final assembly. Since these pieces are so small, it is much safer to cut them by hand rather than on the machine.

Key/Change Tray Fig. 6

This too was made of walnut; the material was dressed to 1/2" in the planer. Even though it may seem feasible, and is possible, planing 3/4" stock to 1/2" on the joiner can leave the work inaccurate, and it can be a hazardous operation.

The tray bottom edges are rabbeted so that they will set into the grooves that are machined into the edges. This edge stock is then mitered, and all the parts are first hand cleaned and then assembled. It will be easier to do it this way instead of having to get the scraper and sanding block into corners. The mitering of the edges, though easily done by hand, is best cut on the bench saw in the jig made for that purpose.

Final Assembly

With all the parts completed and hand cleaned, assembly of the unit can be started. The spacer (Fig. 5) is face glued to the bottom edge of the frame, using two small brads for alignment, and this assembly is then face glued to the bottom edge of the trouser board (Fig. 1). Four No. 6 FHWS are used to secure the three parts together and the entire sub-assembly is set in the clamps. Be certain to use pads (1/4″ ply) where the clamps contact the walnut since their rock maple faces are harder than the walnut. This precaution will avoid the task of removing the burnish marks off the finished walnut surfaces. Once this assembly is taken from the clamps, align the feet in their final position and bore four 3/8″ diameter holes for the dowels. Using glue and the dowels as fasteners, make up the joint.

Next locate the position of the aluminum rod stays (Fig. 3) and drill 1/8″ holes, 1″ deep both in the outer edge of the frame and the trouser board. It is not necessary to find a bit that is a few thousandths larger than the diameter of the rod because the wood will give when the rods are tapped into the holes. Remember not to set these stays permanently now since they will have to be removed in the final stage to be polished and cleaned.

The key/change tray is now joined to the top edge of the back frame with four 3/8″ dowels. Note that these dowels protrude up from the frame 3/8″, and be certain that when the holes are drilled in the tray bottom, the spur of the drill does not pierce through.

With the unit assembled, now is the time to add your trademark. I use a branding iron with my own logo for this purpose, and this operation must be done prior to the beginning of the finishing process.

Finishing the Unit

It is all too common to see projects described in minute detail with no mention of how to finish it. The experienced woodworker, though, is well aware that an expert job of craftmanship is entitled to an equally expert job of finishing.

Wipe all the surfaces with a damp sponge first, let completely dry, and then finish sand these surfaces to remove the minute wood fibers that will soon reveal themselves.

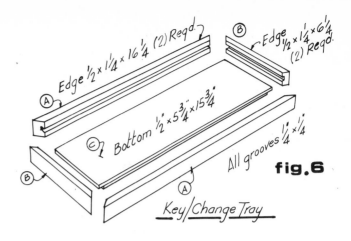

fig.6

Key/Change Tray

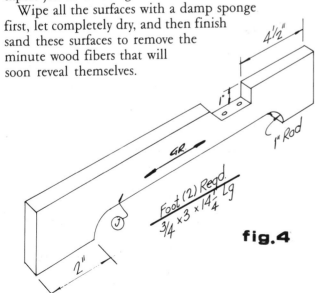

fig.4

Then, using a tac rag, wipe these surfaces clean. I usually mix the natural filler with the stain that I prepare, so this eliminates one step in the finishing process. It is probably a matter of training, but I prefer oil stains over penetrating ones; there seems to be more room for blending with the former, particularly when a rag is used as an applicator. The stain/filler is rubbed into the surface, wiped clean, and then allowed to dry. This material is then set with a coat of white shellac (one pound cut). This step is critical.

Since I ordinarily use a flat alkyd brushing varnish, which is softer than lacquer, I repeat the process with two more coats of shellac over the seal coat, sanding and tac rag wiping between each coat. The last coat of shellac is allowed to dry for two days, and after this time, any burning-in with stick shellac can be done. The final surface is then sanded and wiped clean with the tac rag; now the varnishing can begin.

Varnishing must be done in an area that is constantly heated (70°), dust free, and well ventilated. The ventilation is for your own protection. Of course, it is worth saying that the varnish *must* be the same temperature as the surface to which it is to be applied. Nothing is more frustrating than to find blushing, crazing, or uneven drying because of humidity or sub-standard temperatures. Two coats of varnish are applied, and again, the first coat is sanded and tac rag wiped before the second is applied. The final coat is allowed to dry for two days.

The rubbing process involves the use of wet/dry sandpaper, soaked in lemon oil, followed by a rubbing with steel wood (000), also using lemon oil as a lubricant. Note that this is the first time that steel wool is used in the finishing process; steel fibers are almost impossible to remove from the surface, and if they are trapped under the "skin", they can destroy the appearance of the finishing job. The process described here should produce a surface that has a delicate sheen, while at the same time, amplifies the color and figure of the wood. The unit shown here was finished in this manner.

The almunium stays (Fig.3), left in place all this time, now can be removed, cleaned and polished, then set permanently in place. After the unit has been wiped dry, the felt insert for the tray is installed, a brass hanger set at the back of the frame, and the vinyl "T" edging is pressed into the saw cut at the top edge of the trouser board (Fig. 1). The unit is now complete.

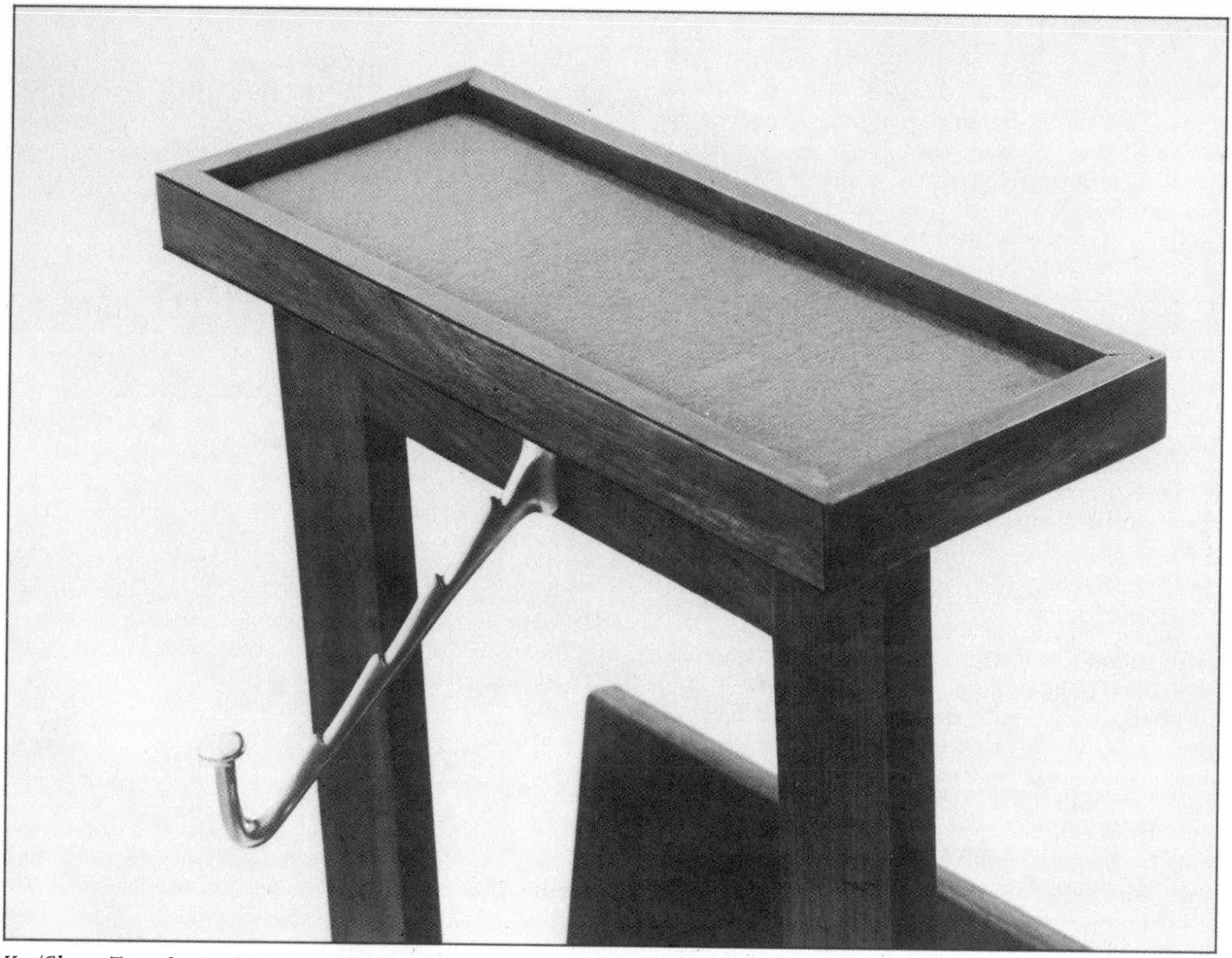

Key/Change Tray...showing fabric covered insert & coat hook at back of frame.

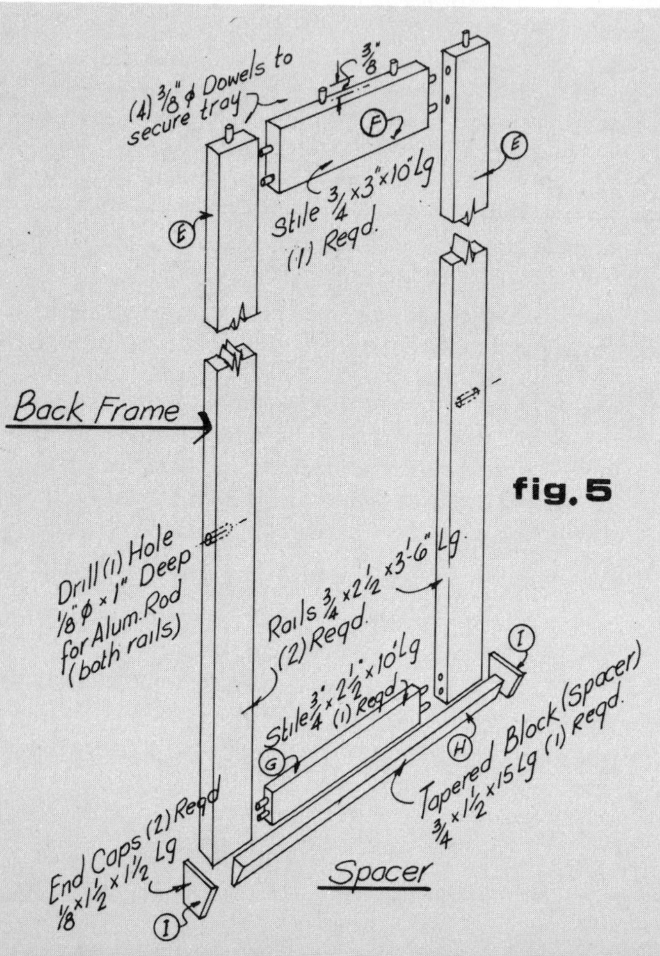

(4) 3/8" ⌀ Dowels to secure tray
3/8"
F
E
Stile 3/4 x 3" x 10" Lg (1) Reqd.
E
Back Frame
fig. 5
Drill (1) Hole 1/8" ⌀ x 1" Deep for Alum. Rod (both rails)
Rails 3/4 x 2 1/2 x 3'-6" Lg. (2) Reqd.
Stile 3/4" x 2 1/2" x 10" Lg (1) Reqd.
I
G
H
Tapered Block (Spacer) 3/4 x 1 1/2 x 15 Lg (1) Reqd.
End Caps (2) Reqd 1/8 x 1 1/2 x 1 1/2 Lg
Spacer
I

MATERIALS LIST

NO.	PCS.		SIZE T	W	L	MATERIAL
A	2	Tray Edge	½	1¼	1′4¼″	Walnut
B	2	Tray Edge	½	1¼	6¼	Walnut
C	1	Tray Bottom	½	5¾	1′3¾″	Walnut
D	1	Tray Insert	⅓	5 1/8	1′3 1/8″	Luon Ply (Felt Covered)
E	2	Frame Rails	¾	2½	3′6″	Walnut
F	1	Stile	¾	3	10″	Walnut
G	1	Stile	¾	2½	10″	Walnut
H	1	Spacer	¾	1½	1′3″	Walnut
I	2	End Caps	1/8	1½	1½″	Walnut
J	2	Feet	¾	3	1′2¼″	Walnut
K	1	Trouser Bd.	¾	1′3¾″	2′9¼″	Walnut
L	1	Trouser Edge			1′3 5/8″	Vinyl 'T' Edge
M	2	Support Rods		1/8	8¼″	Alum. Rod

About The Author:

Bill Marsella is an industrial designer and woodworker living in Lynbrook, New York.

Band Sawn Boxes

by Paul Haines

As unlikely as it may seem there are many fine craftsmen here in the entertainment capital of the world. Hidden in little corners among the glitter of lights and life in the "fast lane" there are those of us who live normal lives and practice our craft as artists and craftsmen, just as those anywhere else.

Myself; a native Las Vegan employed in the local industry for many years needed a creative outlet which was missing in my work. Always into arts and crafts, I found woodworking to be the craft to which I gravitated. Eventually, I dropped the others, unless I incorporated them into my woodwork.

My interest in woodworking has snowballed over a period of 15 years and has been an obsessive interest for the last five of those years. What started out as a hobby has turned into a profession. My work seems to be gaining more acceptance as time goes on. I'm striving for a position where I can quit doing commission work (except when an exciting job comes along) to have enough favorable work to be able to do what I want and have a market for that work.

Wood; being a naturally warm and sensuous material keeps me in continual anticipation of what it will do and how it will react. This anticipation creates energy and excitement while working toward creating an original piece. I've had to learn not to prejudge a piece of work. Many times something unfinished just didn't seem so great, then once completed, turned out to be spectacular.

To me, one of the greatest pleasures is putting the first coat of oil on an original piece. One has to be there and see it for themselves to appreciate that thrill! The problems have been solved, the tedium has ended, its a relaxed time, almost festive. It's like opening a Christmas present. The lifeless object is there, but it hasn't truly come to life. It could be comparable to the stages in the development of a butterfly going from cocoon-like in color to having a vibrant rich life of its own. For the artist-craftsman, the challenges are twofold; design, plus the ability to make that design a reality. While a piece may seem simple, there is a point where one has to stare at a blank piece of paper, find the subject, get it on paper, then make the hundreds of construction and design decisions to finally have the piece become a reality.

I try not to be too rigid in the shape that I impose on the material. I listen to the wood and let it help lead me to the final design. If you go against the wood, your design will never seem natural.

I have no particular philosophy about my work, unless you could call just pure joy in the creative process philosophy. I don't concern myself about trying to make a statement of any kind through my work. I merely strive for a pleasing, creative, well-crafted design.

I like to keep exploring, to avoid getting in a rut, becoming bored with the work (horrors), or just plain burned-out.

At the present time I'm designing and building containers, particularly bandsaw boxes. This technique is fast (usually). It's just letting your imagination run wild. There seems to be few restrictions and the

Curved Lid Box

possibilities are endless. I've made at least 100 boxes; all of them different. Most of these are craft quality. Some are what I like to think of as show quality. I find these boxes to be so much fun to do. They're instant gratification, which most of us as woodworkers need at times between tedius, precision pieces.

I'm doing mostly boxes of consumer quality, as I plan to do three or four good West Coast craft shows a year. I do a series of these boxes in between major commission projects. Occasionally, I create a box of show quality. These boxes are not for sale because I am accumulating a collection to use for show purposes.

I enjoy the exploration of the woodworking processes and want to create designs in which I find pride and satisfaction. Of course, it's a giant plus if these designs enjoy public acceptance. I want very much to be able to point at what I've done with pride. If you need a "break" from more complex projects, or if you need a quick fun project for yourself or as a gift, try one or more of these boxes.

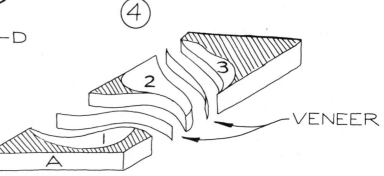

ILLUSTRATION 1

1. Laminate stock to make up block (C).
2. Mill two 3/8'' pieces (B & D). These will be the bottom of the box (D), and the bottom of the lid (B).
3. Mill a ¾'' piece of same dimension for the top of lid (A).

ILLUSTRATION 2

4. Cut body of block (C) in half lengthwise.
5. With the band saw, cut out the shaded area, and discard.
6. Glue body back together.
7. Align body (C) above piece (B) and draw outline of interior onto piece (B) and cut out. This is the bottom of the lid. (See Illustration 5).
8. Glue piece (D) to the bottom of the body (C).

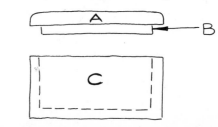

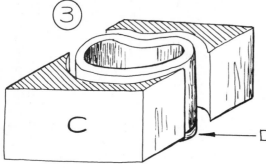

ILLUSTRATION 3

9. Cut the outside off. You now have a rough box with a bottom, but no lid.

ILLUSTRATION 4

10. Draw outline of outside of box onto piece (A), then draw your design inside of this outline.
11. Cut individual sections of this design (1,2, & 3) on band saw.
12. Glue veneer the thickness of band saw kerf to cut line of sections 1 & 3, then clamp this whole assembly back together. (Note: there is no glue between veneer and section 2).
13. When dry, take sections apart again, round and sand all edges dramatically.
14. Now apply glue to free side of veneers and section 2 and clamp all three sections together again.
15. Band saw scrap off outline.

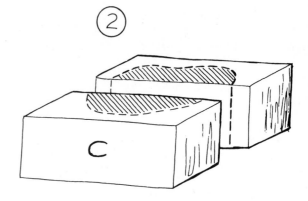

ILLUSTRATION 5

16. Fit and glue piece (B) to the bottom of the lid and you have a perfect fitting lid.

50

CONCH BOX

STEP 1
Draw face of box
on block

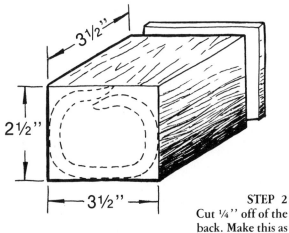

STEP 2
Cut ¼'' off of the
back. Make this as
clean a cut as possible.

BLADE

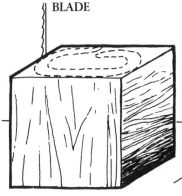

STEP 3
Place block, drawing side up
and cut around outside of drawing with bandsaw.

ENTER HERE

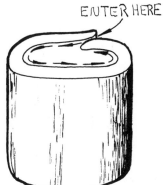

STEP 4
Now, very carefully cut inside out, as
it will become the drawer. Set aside
this piece for use in Step 6.

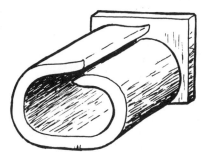

STEP 5
Glue the ¼'' piece back as close to its
original position as possible. Cut with
band saw on the outside circumference
to follow form of box.

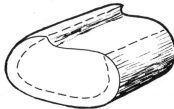

STEP 7
Cut out as indicated, leaving
a shell. Sand the interior,
glue the front and back
pieces back on and you have
your drawer.

STEP 6
Take the piece from Step 4 which will be
the drawer and
cut ¼'' off both
ends. These will
be used in the
next step.

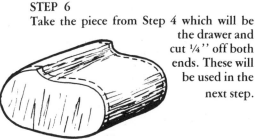

STEP 8
Make a drawer pull, or drill a hole in the back of the box then
glue a button of the same dimensions on the back of the
drawer so drawer can be pushed out from behind. This particular piece is made of walnut and ash, finished with several
coats of oil. The inside of the drawer is finished with a pleas-
ant scented blend of oils (my own formula) as I find that
regular oil tends to leave an unpleasant odor. You may
substitute mineral oil.

BUREAU BOXES

by W. Curtis Johnson

I never thought that I would be interested in making little boxes, but when I read Jim Cummins' article in *Fine Woodworking*, No. 43, I was intrigued. Here was a way to use up all that scrap that had been accumulating around the shop. Some of that scrap had beautiful grain patterns and I didn't want to waste it. I had just developed the wooden hinges presented in *The American Woodworker (Vol. 2, No. 1)* and here

was a chance to use them again. I learned about the "golden ratio" of 0.618 to 1.00 to 1.618, which makes the ratio of the length of the first side to the second side the same as the ratio of the second side to the third. Finally, I was hooked by the same idea that inspired Jim Cummins. Sam Bush of Portland, Oregon had shown how to match the grain on the outside of a box at all four corners in issue No. 32 of *Fine Woodworking*. I had to try it.

Jim Cummins discussed many designs but I have repeatedly built just one that seems to suit my personality. Naturally, I use a number of techniques found in Jim's article but the bureau box described here has enough of my own features to be considered novel. It is designed with wood movement in mind. The bottom is set in a groove. My wooden hinges allow the free floating top to open in either direction or be removed completely. The box has mitered corners with cross-splines to strengthen the joint. It's 3⁷⁄₁₆ by 5⁹⁄₁₆ by 9 inch size follows the golden ratio and is suitable for a bureau top. A tray enlarges the inside area. Recently I have added a small music box movement to brighten the mornings.

Begin by choosing a vertically grained 4/4 board for the sides. In theory it needs to be the height of the box (3 and ³⁄₁₆ inches) by the length of a long plus a short side (14 and ⁷⁄₁₆ inches). In practice, a little extra width will help in matching the grain and

BUREAU BOX

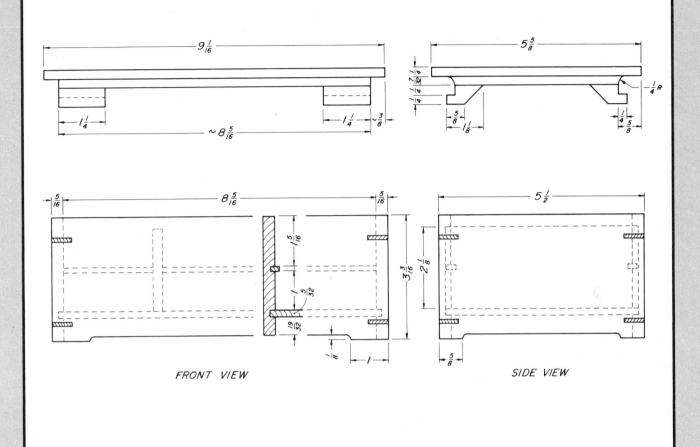

FRONT VIEW

SIDE VIEW

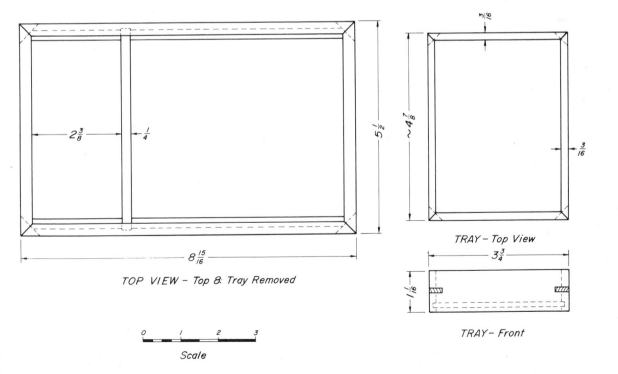

TOP VIEW – Top & Tray Removed

TRAY – Top View

TRAY – Front

Scale

Drawings by Frank Pittman

The completed box with tray and works installed.

Hinge details.

Top view showing use of highly figured wood.

a few extra inches in length will make handling easier and allow for waste in making the miters. I resaw this board on my band saw. Resawing can also be accomplished by ripping on a table saw. However, if you use a table saw for this and other operations, you must take appropriate safety precautions. The inside of the board now becomes the outside, and either way the two new boards are set end to end, they are book matched. Presto, corners made at these ends will be book matched while corners made at the interior of the two boards will naturally match because of the continuous grain.

Smooth the faces of these boards and bring them to the same thickness with a planer, a hand plane, or a jointer. If you choose a jointer, again you must take special safety precautions. Remove the minimum material from the bookmatched faces to retain this feature. A piece of hardwood that is 4/4 when rough is usually surfaced on the two faces to $^{13}/_{16}$ inches in thickness. Careful resawing and planing will yield two $^{5}/_{16}$ inch thick boards, but the actual thickness is irrelevant. Modify the dimensions in the drawing to suit the thickness of your sides.

In keeping with the four matched corners, I like to match the top and bottom of the box by resawing both from a single board. Choose a highly figured scrap. Scraps often include a knot carefully removed from lumber that has become a piece of fine furniture. Tight knots add special interest to a box. For practical reasons it is important to fill any cracks or holes in a knot in the bottom piece, but don't use any filler in the top. Surface the top and bottom to their respective $^{15}/_{32}$ and $^{5}/_{32}$ inch thicknesses, but don't trim them to size just yet.

Use other scraps to make the ¼ by ⅛ inch strips that form the support for the tray. Clearly, this box does not require a music works. If you decide to forego the movement, enlarge the tray to 4 and ⅞ inches square and lower the bottom to ¼ inch from the edge of the sides. If you plan to include the music works, make the divider and the ¼ by ¼ inch trim that will go around the glass covering the music works.

Now we can return to the sides and make the 45 degree cuts for the mitered corners. Although the table saw is the obvious choice for this operation, I prefer my gentler band saw. I then hone perfect miters with my disk sander by setting the table at 45 degrees and attaching a fence. Even if

The completed tray.

The music works.

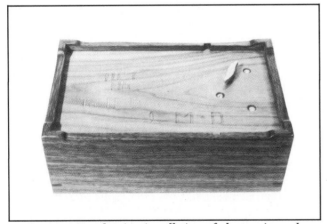

Bottom view showing installation of the music works.

The exact position for the divider will depend on the music works you purchase. Be sure to leave enough room to get it in after the box is assembled. Cut the dado for the divider after you have glued in the supports. You can slide the sides on a scrap so the support does not interfere. Rout from the bottom and stop the dado ¼ inch from the top. You can now remove the material to form the legs on the bottom. The legs greatly improve the volume of the sound when there is a music box movement.

I followed Jim Cummins' ideas when gluing up the mitered sides. Place the sides end to end on a flat surface with the outside up. Hold the three matched corners that are side-by-side tightly together with a piece of masking tape. Now you can fold the box around and check the fit of the divider. Cut the bottom to size leaving a little play for wood movement. Do all of the final sanding on the bottom, the divider, and the insides of the box. Now you are ready to glue the sides together.

With the inside of the sides face up and the three strips of masking tape still in place, paint one side of each miter joint with a minimum of yellow glue. Then paint the other side so that each joint will still have a side wet with glue. Insert the divider and bottom and fold the box together. Tape the fourth corner and place heavy rubber bands around the box to clamp the miters. Check for squareness and put the box aside for the glue to dry. You don't really want too much glue in these joints or it will be a mess to clean up. I put a little more glue in the ''V'' where it will squeeze to the outside, since the outside is easy to clean. With a little practice in painting the glue, only a few small beads will squeeze into the inside, and these are easily knocked off after they dry.

I now trim the top so it is ⅛ inch larger than the box in each dimension for a 1/16 inch overhang. Cut the 7/32 inch deep rabbets in the top so it fits into the box with 1/64 of an inch of play. I create the ¼ inch round rabbet that will become part of the hinge with a router and a router table and a ½ inch core box bit. Use a strip of ½ inch by 1 and ¼ inch wood to make a length of material which will become the other part of the hinge. Rout an extra deep groove because you will trim the hinge to fit the box after it is glued to the top. Cut 1 and ¼ inch long hinges from the length of shaped wood and glue them in place. After the glue is dry, trim the edges of the hinges until the top fits inside the box with about 1/64 of an inch of play.

Whether you cut the ⅛ inch grooves for the cross-splines that strengthen the miter joints on a table saw or a router table, you will have to construct a jig. Cut a ''V'' in a 2 × 4 to hold the box in the proper position. I place two splines on each miter joint about ½ inch from each edge. The cross-splines themselves should fit snugly but not tightly, or you will have trouble getting them in after applying the glue. After the glue has dried, trim the splines flush with the sides using a small saw with no set and a small hand plane.

The tray is constructed in exactly the same way as the box, although only one cross-spline is used in each miter joint. Build the tray only after the box is complete so you can fit it to the finished dimensions of your particular box. The reader will see how the construction sequence described here allows fitting each new part to the foregoing parts in order that precise dimensions become irrelevant.

Sand all the pieces smooth and round the corners slightly. The edges of the hinges should be rounded to work

the angles are correct, the miter joints will fit precisely only if opposite sides are exactly the same length. This is easy to control with a disc sander. Bring the sides to the proper width, keeping in mind that you may need to offset the sides slightly to get the grain to match at each corner.

Now we are ready to cut the grooves. While the versatile table saw can perform this operation, I prefer a router mounted under a table. I rout the groove to fit the mating piece, since this can be done so precisely by adjusting the fence for successive cuts, but of course, you can surface the mating pieces to fit precut grooves. Rout for the bottom on the inside of all four sides, but the tray supports and divider fit only into the long sides.

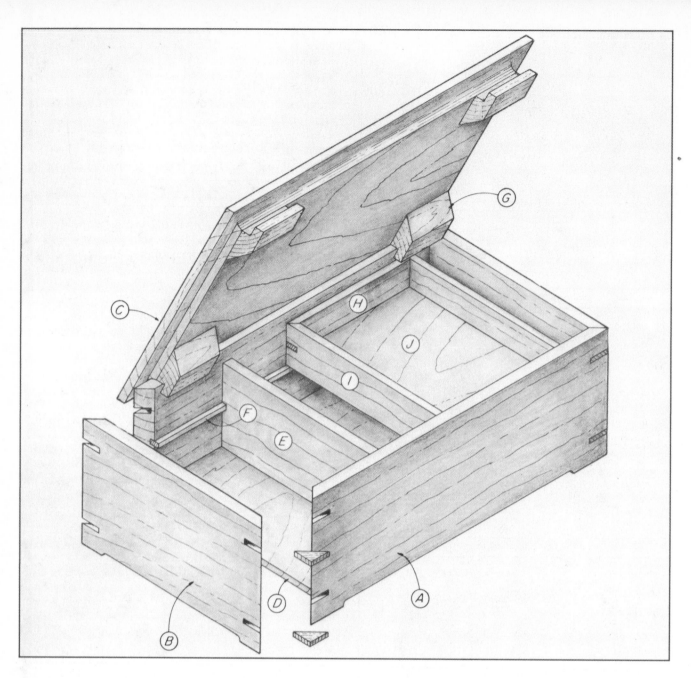

smoothly. First, finish the tray and the inside of the box with two coats of mineral oil. Standard finishes are not recommended because the smell will linger for years. Finish the outside with a standard furniture finish.

Only after the box is completely finished do I drill the holes for the music box works. Measure and drill the holes for the release lever and the winding key. Then the works can be inserted and the mounting holes marked with the movement in place. I turned a little wooden knob with a hole that just fits on the release lever, but properly positioned, the lever will protrude slightly through the side of the box, so this is not absolutely necessary.

Go to your local glazier for a piece of glass to protect the movement. Miter the molding that will hold the glass in place and glue it in with a few small dabs of silicon seal. The molding can then be removed to service the music works.

Music box works are available from many of the companies that sell clock movements. I like the more expensive works that feature steel pins individually set into brass cylinders. Although these are readily available in larger

sizes, I have found the small 22-note movement used here only through Craft Products, 2200 Dean Street, St. Charles IL 60174. The less expensive 18-note movements with a cast brass cylinder are also readily available. Other companies I have found that sell music box movements are listed below: Constantine's, 2050 Eastchester Road, Bronx, NY 10461; Klockit, P.O. Box 629, Lake Geneva, WI 53147; Marshall-Swartchild, 2040 Milwaukee Avenue, Chicago, IL 60647; Mason and Sullivan, 586 Higgins Crowell Road, West Yarmouth, Cape Cod, MA 02673; Turncraft Clock Imports, 7912 Olson Highway 55, Golden Valley, MN 55427-4593; The Woodworkers' Store, 21801 Industrial Boulevard, Rogers, MN 55374.

The box described here could be used to hold a large 72-note music movement. I made such a symphonic quality music box to commemorate my parents' 50th wedding anniversary.

ABOUT THE AUTHOR:
*W. Curtis Johnson is a contributing editor to **The American Woodworker**.*

THE MINIATURE DOVETAIL CHEST

by Nicholas Cavagnaro

When I was a child, my grandparents lived at home with us. My grandfather, who repaired many things around the home, also designed and built simple pieces of furniture. He had no power tools and built with scrap lumber scavenged from crates, construction sites, and friends. Several miniature chests-of-drawers adorned our home in various places and served various functions. I remember my dad used one to organize paid and unpaid bills and other correspondence (he still uses it today). My grandfather had one filled with jewelry, pens and pencils, a magnifying glass, and many important papers. There was a chest of drawers over the bench in the garage filled with small tools and screws and bolts. A farmer friend of my grandfather persuaded him to build one for his home.

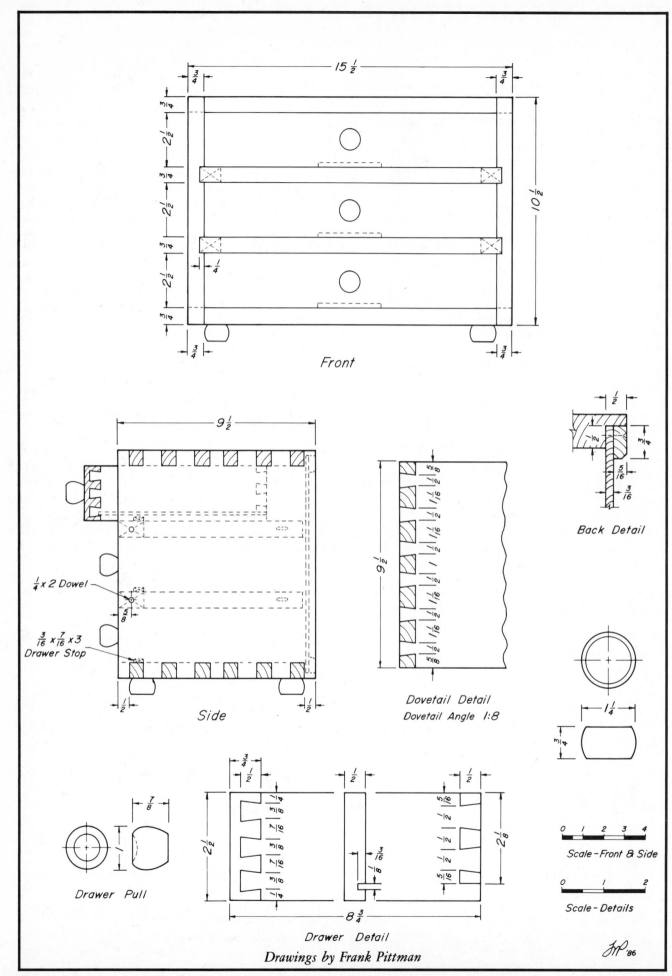

Front

Side

$\frac{1}{4} \times 2$ Dowel

$\frac{3}{16} \times \frac{7}{16} \times 3$
Drawer Stop

Dovetail Detail
Dovetail Angle 1:8

Back Detail

Drawer Pull

Drawer Detail

Scale—Front & Side

Scale—Details

Drawings by Frank Pittman

I began my woodworking experience watching my grandfather at his bench. Everything was done by hand. I was amazed at what he could do and would watch him for hours. When I grew older, I made several miniature chests designed just as my grandfather made them. As I became more and more knowledgeable in woodworking, I decided to improve on the design. My grandfather's chests were constructed with dado, rabbet, and butt joints. I began to design and build miniature chests of hardwood constructed with hand-cut dovetail joinery.

The very first dovetailed miniature chest I built was of red oak. It looked very fine and functioned perfectly. However, I was distracted by the scribe lines visible on the exterior, left over from marking out the dovetails. I told myself that they were the signs of hand-cut dovetails, and for a while this satisfied me. But when someone who saw the chest inadvertently mentioned the lines to me, I knew I had to find a better way.

For a long time the solution eluded me. I thought about scraping and sanding until the lines disappeared, but this was too much work. Finally the answer, so simple, came to me. Scribe all the way across on the inside only. Then mark out the pins on the end grain. Transfer the pin marks down with a square and a fine pencil on the inside and outside. Then scribe *between the pins only* on the exterior. Saw and chop out the spaces between the pins, then scribe around them to mark the tails. Transfer the tail markings to the end grain with a square and fine pencil. Then, using a dovetail gauge and a pencil, mark the exterior side. Now scribe *between the tails only* on the exterior side. Saw from the inside, being careful not to cut below the scribe mark on the exterior side. Chop out the pieces between the tails.

Building the miniature chests is a challenge. The dovetails are very visible and must be well executed to be pleasing to the eye. Minor imperfections in fit can be filled with veneer slivers glued and driven in. If the imperfections are few and small, the repair will be invisible as well as permanent.

Miniature chests are a perfect project to utilize a small quantity of highly figured or difficult-to-work wood. I have come to view them for myself, at least, as the ultimate test of craftsmanship and skill, and I save the most beautiful and figured woods to build them with. Walnut and cherry are my favorite woods because they scribe well and are strong in grain to withstand a tight drive fit. Red oak is difficult to scribe accurately. It is hard to follow your marks in the coarse, open grain, and the scriber wants to wander from the harder grain to the softer grain.

The first step in making a miniature chest is to edge-glue the boards for the two sides and the top and bottom. Next, hand plane the boards perfectly flat and parallel on both sides. This is essential for an accurate fit of the dovetails. After planing, cut the boards to length and width. Dado the sides for the runners and rails to fit in. I rip the sides slightly wider prior to dadoing and then recut after dadoing to remove any tear out from the dado as it leaves the cut.

Now, cut the rabbet grooves for the rear panel and mouldings to fit in. These are stopped rabbets, and you will have to cut the corners with a chisel after the carcase is assembled. Cutting the stopped rabbets is not dangerous; it just takes concentration. Use a wooden fence attached to the rip fence. When the dado is set to the right height and width, mark the beginning and end of the blade against the wooden fence with a pencil so you will know where the blade will begin and end cutting. Lower the board onto the moving blade while holding it against the fence, making sure that you begin your cut behind the scribe lines for the dovetails. Move the board along and then lift it off the blade before you get to the scribe marks on the other end of the board.

Mark out and cut the dovetails. Then, assemble the carcase, having first checked the fit of the dovetails. Never try the dovetails all the way when checking. If they will start and go together 1/6 to 1/4 the way, you know they will go all the way. You should have to hammer them together with considerable force using a wooden block, of course. When the assembly is dry, clean off the protruding pins and tails with a razor sharp block plane.

Drawer runners fit in shallow dados. The runners are set in 1¼" from the front of the chest, glued for the first 1½" only, then held in place with a screw and washer through an oval expansion slot in the rear. Rails are set in next and

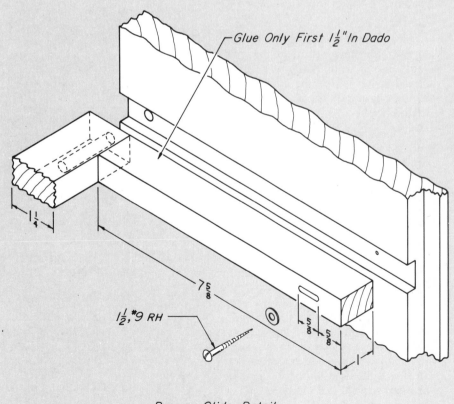

Drawer Slide Detail

pinned from the sides with ¼" x 2" dowels. The runners and rails are fitted to the dado grooves by planing from a slightly oversize piece.

> ## "For drawer knobs, I prefer to turn my own. The variations are infinite."

The back of the chest is 3/16" plywood of the same wood as the chest. It fits in the rabbet cut in the back and is glued in place, with mouldings glued and bradded over it in the rabbet. The mouldings fit slightly proud of the surface. The brad heads are set and when the glue is dry and the clamps are removed, the mouldings are planed flush. Then, with a razor sharp knife, carve a slight chamfer all about on the inner edge of the moulding. Use stick shellac to fill the brad holes and any minor imperfections.

Drawers for the miniature chest are dovetailed front and rear. They are made for a tight fit, then worked down with plane and sandpaper to a perfect gliding fit. The sides and front are grooved for the bottom panel (1/8" doorskin material). Drawer stops are attached to the rails.

For drawer knobs, I prefer to turn my own. The variations are infinite. You could also carve the knobs. The main consideration is that the knob fit the hand easily and comfortably to perform its task well.

Plane, scrape, and sand the chest and drawer fronts to 220 grit. Then finish everything inside and out with Danish oil on the first application. On the second application, oil the exterior only. Finish off with wax and 400 grit sandpaper.

Drawer sides, runners, and kickers should be paste waxed to increase the glide of the drawers. Keep the miniature chest empty for the first month or so. Try the drawers often. If, after a week or so, a drawer doesn't glide just right, find the friction spot and work it down with scraper or sandpaper. Re-oil and re-wax. Only when you are satisfied that all is well should a miniature chest be put into service. The successive owners will appreciate your efforts. Like a fine wine, this piece of furniture should not serve before its time.

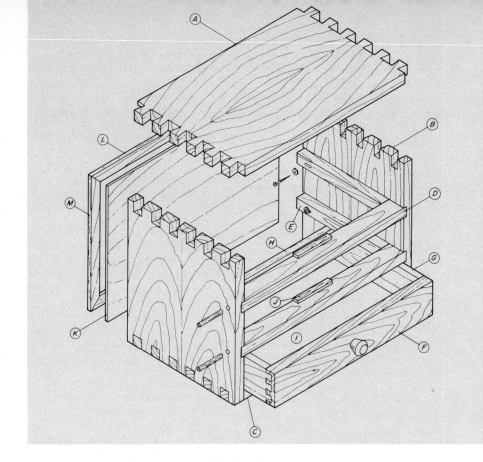

BILL OF MATERIAL

Code	Description	Quan.	T	W	L
A	Top	1	¾	9½	15½
B	Side	2	¾	9½	10½
C	Bottom	1	¾	9½	15½
D	Front Rail	2	¾	1¼	14½
E	Drawer Slide	4	¾	1	7 5/8
F	Drawer Front	3	¾	2½	14
G	Drawer Side	6	½	2½	8¾
H	Drawer Back	3	½	2 1/8	14
I	Drawer Bottom	3	1/8	8 9/16	13 5/8
J	Drawer Stop	3	3/16	7/16	3
K	Back	1	3/16	10	15
L	Back Frame - Top & Bottom	2	5/16	¾	15
M	Back Frame - Ends	2	5/16	¾	10

ABOUT THE AUTHOR

Nicholas Cavagnaro has worked as a forester, surveyor, road design and logging camp foreman. He presently owns and operates his own woodworking business in Orofino, Idaho.

Miniature Blanket Chest

by John A. Nelson

T he original of this extraordinary small blanket chest was found in Pennsylvania and was made around 1820. Made of pine and poplar, it is only 16″ wide, 10½″ deep and 12″ high. The original blanket chest had an imaginative, painted grain effect. Today, this small chest could be used as a jewelry box, a document box or a hundred other small storage uses. Exact hardware, as noted on the drawing, can be purchased today, right out of stock so your "copy" will be very close to the original. The "copy" of the chest in the photograph was made of mahogany only because that was the only kind of wood I had available the day I was going to make it. I distressed it slightly and painted it an early powder plue paint in keeping with an early color shade that was popular at the time this chest was made. This

chest is rather easy to make and can be made in a weekend or so with no problem at all.

Instructions

As with any project, carefully study the illustrations so you will fully understand exactly how the chest goes together. Figure 1 illustrates the front view, right side view and the top view of the chest as completed. Figure 2 illustrates the first sub-assembly of the case and lid, and Figure 3 illustrates the final case assembly. Figure 4 illustrates how the two drawers are made and assembled.

Refer to the bill of materials and note that most of the primary wood must be planed down to a 3/8″ thickness. Cut all pieces to basic sizes and glue up extra width material, if necessary. As the maximum width board is 9½″, this may not be necessary. Notice, the drawer front is the only piece

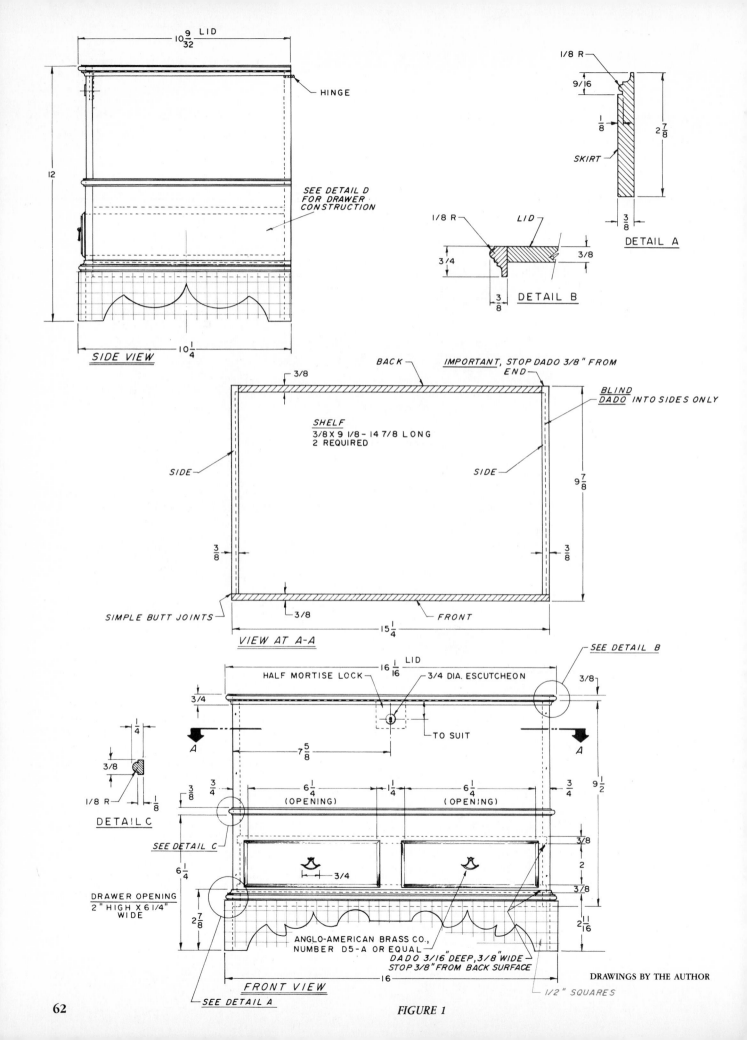

FIGURE 1

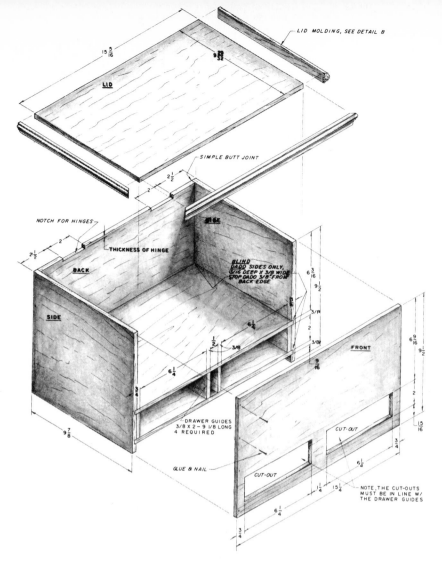

LID MOLDING, SEE DETAIL B

15 5/16

LID

SIMPLE BUTT JOINT

2 1/2

2

NOTCH FOR HINGES

SIDE

THICKNESS OF HINGE

2 1/2   2

BACK

SIDE

BLIND
DADO SIDES ONLY.
3/16 DEEP X 3/8 WIDE
STOP DADO 3/8" FROM
BACK EDGE

6 3/16

9 1/2

3/8

2

3/8

6 1/4

1/2   3/8

6 1/4

FRONT

6 9/16

9 1/2

DRAWER GUIDES
3/8 X 2 — 9 1/8 LONG
4 REQUIRED

GLUE & NAIL

9 7/8

CUT-OUT

CUT-OUT

6 1/4

6 1/4

1 1/4   15 1/4

3/4

15
16

3/4

NOTE, THE CUT-OUTS
MUST BE IN LINE W/
THE DRAWER GUIDES

FIGURE 2

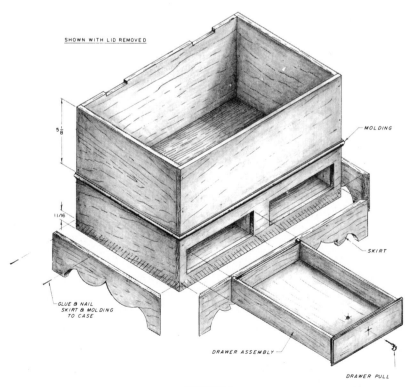

SHOWN WITH LID REMOVED

5 1/8

MOLDING

11/16

SKIRT

GLUE & NAIL
SKIRT & MOLDING
TO CASE

DRAWER ASSEMBLY

DRAWER PULL

FIGURE 3

of primary wood that is ½" thick. Cut all molding to approximate size using either a router or a shaper. See details A, B and C, of Figure 1.

Dado the two sides 3/16" deep and 3/8" wide as shown stopping 3/8" from the back surface. Assemble the two side panels, the back panel, the shelf and bottom boards and four drawer guides as shown in the top view of Figure 2 with glue and square-cut nails. Take care to keep everything square and flush. Add to this sub-assembly the front panel and be sure that the two drawer openings in the front panel line up exactly with the two drawer openings. Glue and nail it in place as shown. Carefully sand all surfaces keeping square corners at all times.

Fit the lid to the case assembly and add the lid molding as shown at detail B, Figure 1. Notch the back board for the hinge and temporarily attach hinges to the lid and case to check for correct fit. Mortise for the lock and catch as needed and, if all fits correctly, remove the hinges from the lid and case and remove the lock and catch to ready the case and lid for finishing.

Add the center molding 5 1/8" down from the top and add the skirt 11/16" up as shown in Figure 3. Using the router or shaper, cut the 3/16" radius on all four sides of the drawer front and notch the ends ¼" deep by 3/8". See detail D, Figure 4. Dado the drawer front, sides and back as shown per Figure 4. Dry fit all pieces and if correct, assemble, keeping everything square. Do not glue the drawer bottom in place so as to allow for expansion of the wood. Check to see that the drawer assemblies slide into the drawer openings freely. Drill for drawer pulls as shown and add to drawer.

Finishing

As noted above, the original chest had a painted grain finish, so to be one hundred percent authentic, your "copy" probably should have a painted grain finish. In reality, this chest will look very nice with a simple stain finish or painted like the chest in the photograph. Add the lock, catch, escutcheon plate and the two hinges. You now have an "antique" miniature chest to enjoy for years to come.

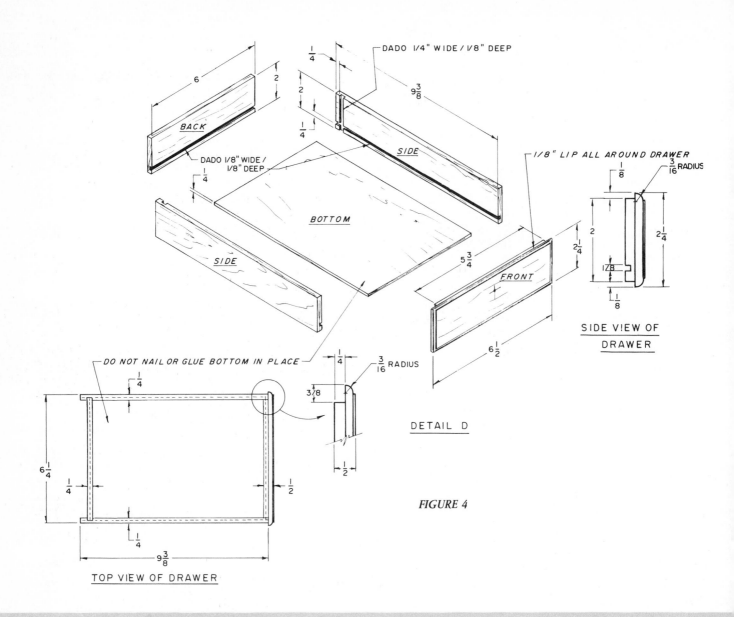

FIGURE 4

Vendors List

Square cut nails from Tremont Nail Co., 21 Elm Street, P.O. Box 111, Wareham, MA 02571.

Paint (if used) from Stulb Paint and Chemical Co., P.O. Box 297, Norristown, PA 19404 (write or call, 1-800-211-8444, for their color card).

Brasses from Anglo-American Brass Co., 4146 Mitzi Drive, Box 9792, San Jose, CA 95157-0792.

MATERIAL LIST		
PART	SIZE	REQ'D
SIDE PANEL	3/8 X 9 1/2 – 9 7/8 LONG	2
FRONT PANEL	3/8 X 9 1/2 – 15 1/4 LONG	1
BACK PANEL	3/8 X 9 1/2 – 14 1/2 LONG	1
SHELF / BOTTOM	3/8 X 9 1/8 – 14 7/8 LONG	2
DRAWER GUIDE	3/8 X 2 – 9 1/8 LONG	4
LID	3/8 X 9 29/32 – 15 5/16 LONG	1
LID MOLDING	3/8 X 3/4 – 40 LONG	1
CENTER MOLDING	1/4 X 3/8 – 40 LONG	1
SKIRT	3/8 X 2 7/8 – 40 LONG	1
FRONT – DRAWER	1/2 X 2 1/4 – 6 1/2 LONG	1
SIDE – DRAWER	1/4 X 2 – 9 3/8 LONG	2
BACK – DRAWER	1/4 X 2 – 6 LONG	1
BOTTOM – DRAWER	1/8 X 6 – 8 3/4 LONG	1
HINGE – BRASS	1/2 (1") X 2 LONG	2
DRAW PULL	3/4" WIDE – BRASS	2
MORTISE LOCK	FOR LID	1
SQUARE-CUT NAIL	3/4" LONG	60

About The Author
John A. Nelson is a contributing editor to **The American Woodworker**.

Traditional Chest

by W. Curtis Johnson

The top has a novel hinge which allows the top to stand open or be removed completely.

This traditional chest uses just six wide boards and is constructed so that it is unaffected by wood movement.

This chest is not only a storage box, but it may serve as a seat or a table as well. Its dimensions are 30 inches long, 15 inches wide, and 15 inches high; so it has the shape of two cubes set side by side. It has the traditional six-board design discussed by Franklin H. Gottshall in his article *"Carcase Construction," The American Woodworker,* volume 1, number 3.

My early furniture used cross-grain construction,

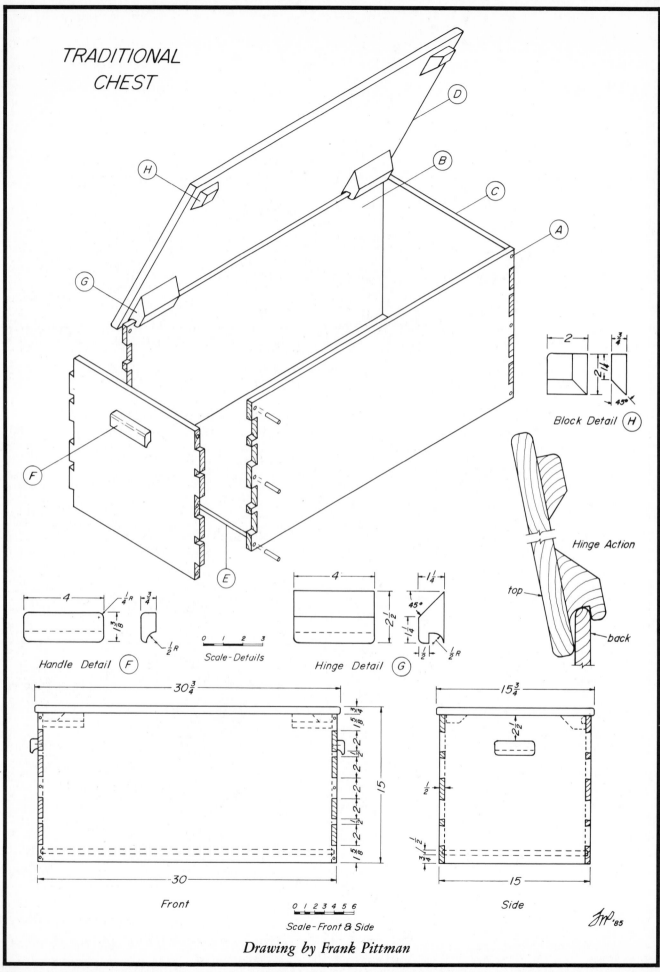

TRADITIONAL
CHEST

H

D

B

C

A

G

F

E

Block Detail H

2

3/4

2 1/4

45°

Hinge Action

top

back

Handle Detail F

4

1/4 R

3/4

1 3/8

1/2 R

Scale-Details

0 1 2 3

Hinge Detail G

4

1 1/4

45°

1/4

2 1/2

1/2

1/2 R

30 3/4

30

3/4

5/8

1 1/4

2

2

2

2

2

2

2

1 1/4

1 5/8

15

Front

15 3/4

2 1/2

1/2

1/2

3/4

15

Side

0 1 2 3 4 5 6
Scale-Front & Side

Drawing by Frank Pittman

JP '85

and the wood in some of these pieces has now split. Thus, I am particularly sensitive to wood movement, and I prefer simple designs that avoid this problem. Here, there is no joint where the grain of one board is glued across the grain of another. Through dovetails are used for decoration and for their superior strength in joining the sides at their end grain. The bottom floats in a groove, free to expand and contract with humidity. The top is completely free even without metal hinges to hold one side down.

Begin by carefully selecting and dimensioning your wood. Since each piece is wide, you will undoubtedly have to glue-up your boards. The top was made by matching two lengths cut from the same 9 inch wide 4/4 board. Another way to match the grain for each glued-up piece is to resaw thick stock on a band saw. My supplier had some fine 6/4 walnut in 8 inch widths, so I chose this wood for the sides. Resawed and dimensioned, this lumber ultimately yielded sides that were 1/2 inch thick. Thicker sides dimensioned to 3/4 inches from standard 4/4 lumber would have worked just as well. I chose red cedar for the bottom because I prefer solid wood, and cedar is relatively stable. You could also use the wood you have chosen for the top and sides, or a good grade of hardwood plywood.

Readers with a well equipped shop will have no trouble dimensioning the lumber. However, a table saw and a sharp hand plane are sufficient for the task if your lumber is already surfaced on the two faces. Use the table saw to straighten the edges of the lumber to be glued into a wider board. Place the two boards to be joined in your vise with the top faces together and the two edges that are to mate side by side. Plane both edges at the same time, checking to be sure they are straight. Prepared in this way, the two boards will mate perfectly, even if the edges are not perpendicular to the face. Glue your boards to form the wide pieces. A sharp hand plane is a joy to use, and it will smooth the surfaces of each piece after they are glued-up. I made three chests in this run and surfaced the boards for each one of them with my trusty jack plane.

With the sides sanded smooth and cut to size, you are ready to saw the dovetails. This procedure has been described in a number of articles in *The American Woodworker*, as well as

The hinge uses the top of the rear panel as the pivot.

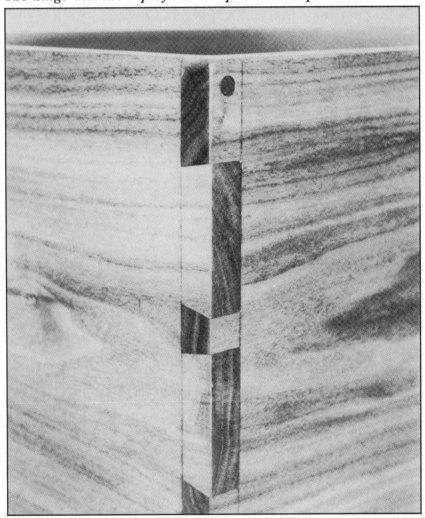

Through dovetail joints are a particularly sturdy way to join the sides at the end grain. The depth line was retained to add to the decoration provided by the dovetails. The dowels give extra strength at critical points.

The simple wooden handle is secured with two brass screws.

elsewhere. I scribed the depth line deeply and retained it for decoration. I also used a minimum number of pins and varied their size to add interest to the joint. The pins were cut on the front and rear panels and the tails on the ends. Since the ends then slide onto the front and rear, this gives the greatest strength for forces against the larger areas.

Before assembling the sides, you must cut a groove for the bottom in each side. Be sure to stop the groove in the front and rear panels so it won't show at the ends. Size the bottom so it has sufficient play across the grain for wood movement. Check to make sure everything fits, and then with the bottom in place, permanently assemble the dovetails with glue. Don't glue in the bottom as it is meant to be free floating to allow for wood movement. At this point, I drilled a 1/4 inch hole in each large pin and put three walnut dowels in each dovetail joint. This prevents the ends from sliding off even if the glue fails, but more importantly, it gives extra strength at the corners. At the bottom, the dowels will prevent the joint from separating should the chest be dragged across the floor. At the top, the dowels will add strength where the top hinges.

As far as I can tell, the hinges used here are novel. I have never liked metal hinges with a heavy top because eventually the screws pull out. Also, if the top warps, they hold the front end open. These hinges use the edge of the rear panel as the pivot and are constructed so the top can stand open. Since the top is not attached to the chest, it can be removed completely. If the top warps slightly, it can find its own equilibrium position.

The hinges are made from two 4/4 pieces and then glued to the top. Refer to the detail in the drawing to understand their operation and review their dimensions. Clamp two pieces which are 4 inches long and more than 5 inches wide face to face. Drill a one inch hole in the center into the end grain through the entire four inches. This gives a 1/2 inch radius, semicircular groove along the grain in the face of each board. Saw both boards along the center of the groove to create four pieces with a 1/2 inch radius removed from one corner. Two of these pieces will become the handles. Simply cut them to a 1 3/8 inch width and round all the edges and corners except

those that will join the ends. The handles are attached with brass screws about 2 1/2 inches from the top. The other two pieces need to be resawn to a 1/2 inch thickness so the 1/2 inch radius tapers to a sharp edge. Next, cut a 1/4 by 1/2 inch rabbet along the grain in one edge of two pieces, each 4 inches long and 2 inches wide. If your sides are thicker than 1/2 inch, your rabbet will have to be wider and your lumber correspondingly thicker. If in doubt, construct the hinge from scrap lumber to check out its operation before committing your expensive top. You will see that there is a great deal of leeway in the design. Glue the faces of the two pieces together with the edge of the rabbet at the 90 degree edge of the radius. Cut the 45 degree angle and round the edges and corners except those that will face the top. *(Figure 1)*

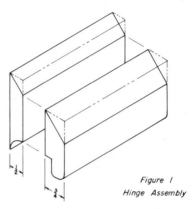

Figure 1
Hinge Assembly

The top itself should overhang on all sides about 3/8 of an inch. Give the top edges a 1/4 inch radius for the comfort of those who sit on it. When it is completely sanded, you are ready to glue on the hinges. Be sure to maintain the overhang and allow 1/16 of an inch of play from side to side. Finally, make and glue the blocks at the front which position the top. There should be 1/8 of an inch of play from front to rear to allow for expansion across the grain with higher humidity. If the humidity has already been high for some time, 1/16 of an inch of play should be sufficient. Note that the top will open in both directions if the hinge mechanism is placed at all four corners.

Finish the inside (but not a cedar bottom) with mineral oil from your local drug store. Don't use a standard finish as the inside will always emit that particular odor. Finish the outside to your taste. I used an oil finish here.

BILL OF MATERIALS

(A) 1 Front 1/2″ × 14 3/4″ × 30″
(B) 1 Back 1/2″ × 14 3/4″ × 30″
(C) 2 Sides 1/2″ × 14 3/4″ × 15″
(D) 1 Top 3/4″ × 15 3/4″ × 30 3/4″
(E) 1 Bottom 1/2″ × 14 1/2″ × 29 1/2″
(F) 2 Handles 3/4″ × 1 3/8″ × 4″
(G) 2 Hinges 3/4″ × 2 1/2″ × 4″ and 3/4″ × 2″ × 4″
(H) 2 Front Blocks 3/4″ × 2″ × 2″

About the Author

W. Curtis Johnson is a contributing editor to The American Woodworker.

Bathroom Shelf

by John A. Nelson

This very simple bathroom shelf would make an excellent project for your son, daughter or grandchild to make with you. A project such as this one could get them started in woodworking. This shelf also makes an excellent crafts show item as it can be made in an evening with very little material.

As with any project, study the drawings so you understand how it all goes together. Cut all pieces to size per the bill of materials. Sand all parts on all sides and edges.

Lay out and cut the back, part 1, the shelf, part 2, and the two side pieces, part 3, per the illustration. It is a good idea to cut out and sand the two sides while tacked together. Also, while the two sides are still tacked together, locate and drill the two ½" diameter holes for the rods, part 5.

Assemble the back to the shelf and attach the two sides, keeping everything square. Center the two braces, part 4, with the sides and leave a ¼" overhang on the sides and bottom as shown. Add the two rods and the shelf is complete!

A simple clear finish, as the one shown in the photograph, is all that is needed to complete the shelf.

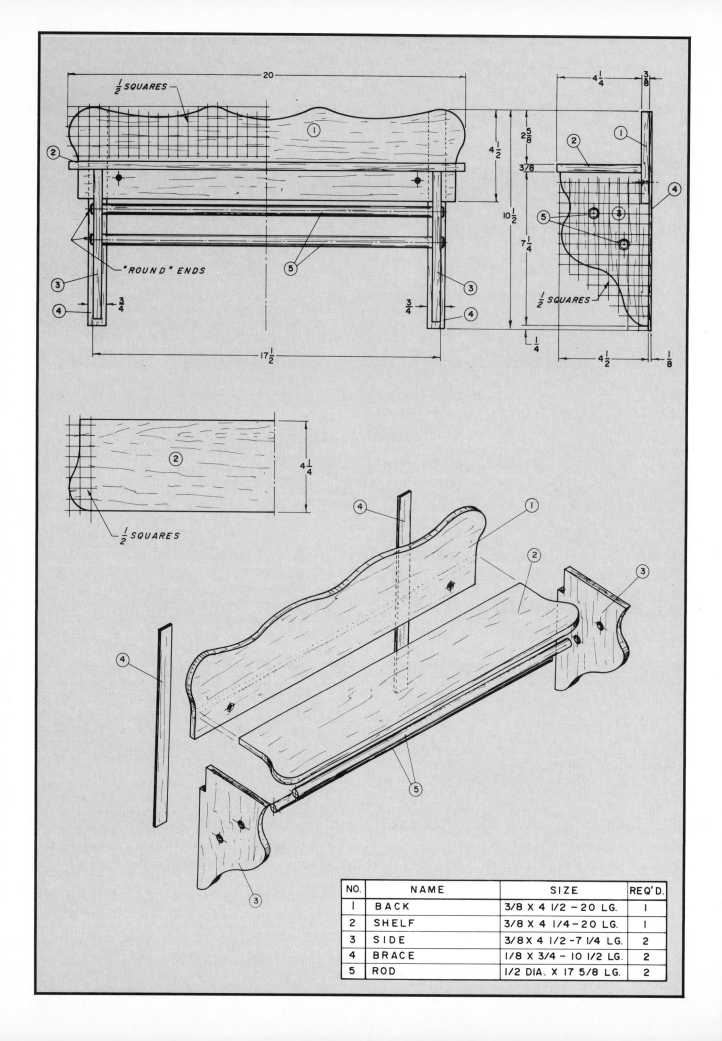

NO.	NAME	SIZE	REQ'D.
1	BACK	3/8 X 4 1/2 – 20 LG.	1
2	SHELF	3/8 X 4 1/4 – 20 LG.	1
3	SIDE	3/8 X 4 1/2 – 7 1/4 LG.	2
4	BRACE	1/8 X 3/4 – 10 1/2 LG.	2
5	ROD	1/2 DIA. X 17 5/8 LG.	2

Towel & Tissue Rack

by John A. Nelson

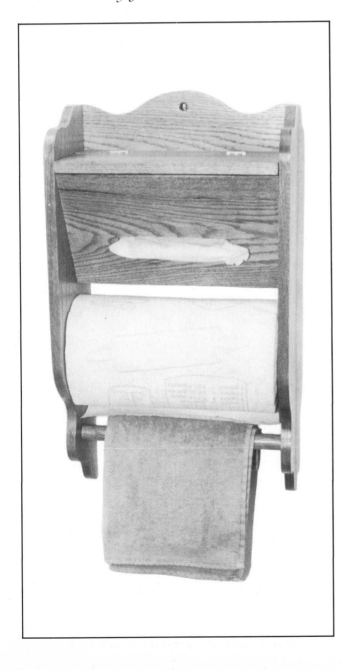

This handy kitchen or bathroom rack provides a convenient place to store a large paper towel roll, a medium size tissue box and a cloth towel—all centrally located. This project can be made of almost any kind of wood from soft pine to hard oak—the one in the photo is made of white oak.

Rough cut all parts per the bill of materials and sand all over. On a sheet of paper or cardboard draw out a one inch grid and, point for point, transfer the shape of the side, part 1, to the sheet. Locate the center of the two 1" diameter holes for the two bars. On the sheet, carefully lay out the location for the support, part 3.

Temporarily tack the two sides together with small finish nails and transfer the shape of the side from the paper to the wood. Locate and drill two small 1/32" diameter holes through the two parts to exactly locate the two 1" diameter holes that will be added later. Cut out the sides and sand all edges before separating the two sides.

On the inside surface of the sides and from the center of the two 1/32" diameter holes, drill the two 1" diameter holes 1/4" deep. Be sure you have a matching pair and take care not to drill through the sides. On the inside surfaces of the sides carefully locate and draw the exact location of where the support will be located.

Carefully lay out and transfer the shape of the top of the top back, part 2, per the illustration and cut out. Note the bottom edge of part 2 is cut at 25 degrees.

Lay out and cut out the two supports and glue them in place on the sides. Be sure both are identical and that they are located in the exact same place in the sides. Put aside to let the glue set.

Cut the bottom, part 4, and the face board, part 5, to the given size. Note the 25 degree angular cut. Locate and drill two 1/2" diameter holes in the face board for the slot 2 3/4" up from the bottom and 2 1/4" in from the two sides. Cut out the slot between the two 1/2" diameter holes.

Cut the top board, part 6, and the lid, part 7. Notch the top board for the two hinges, part 12. Add hinges to the two parts to check for a correct fit. If everything is correct, remove the hinges at this time.

Cut the bottom bar, part 8, to length and chamfer the ends slightly.

Turn the end of the middle bar, part 9. Note this part has a 1/2" diameter shoulder 2 5/8" long. Drill a 1/2" diameter hole 3" deep into the matching middle bar, part 10. Chamfer the ends of both bars slightly.

Nail and glue the top back, part 2, in place using the support, part 3, as a guide. Attach the top board, part 6, in place, again using part 3 as a guide. The face board and bottom are added to the assembly, also using the support as a guide. Don't forget to put the bottom bar, part 8, in place before you glue and nail everything together. Take care not to get any glue on the finished surfaces. Wipe off any extra glue.

Attach the lid, part 7, using the two hinges. Check for a good fit. Check the fit for the middle bar and spring, parts 9, 10 and 11. Adjust if necessary—you want a snug fit but not a tight fit. Sand all surfaces keeping all edges sharp.

Finish this project using your favorite stain and top coat.

This Towel and Tissue Rack will make a great addition to your workshop, too. It would be nice, just once, to have a paper towel handy whenever you need one in your shop. I know I can never find anything to wipe my hands on but my pants.

Just ask my wife Joyce!

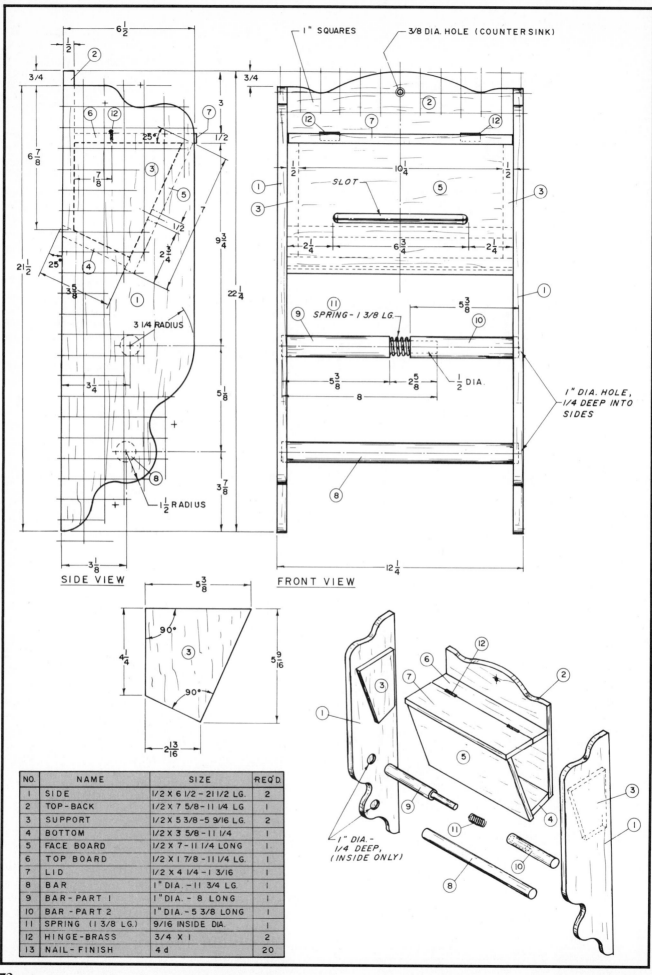

NO.	NAME	SIZE	REQ'D.
1	SIDE	1/2 X 6 1/2 - 21 1/2 LG.	2
2	TOP-BACK	1/2 X 7 5/8 - 11 1/4 LG	1
3	SUPPORT	1/2 X 5 3/8 - 5 9/16 LG.	2
4	BOTTOM	1/2 X 3 5/8 - 11 1/4	1
5	FACE BOARD	1/2 X 7 - 11 1/4 LONG	1
6	TOP BOARD	1/2 X 1 7/8 - 11 1/4 LG.	1
7	LID	1/2 X 4 1/4 - 1 3/16	1
8	BAR	1" DIA. - 11 3/4 LG.	1
9	BAR - PART 1	1" DIA. - 8 LONG	1
10	BAR - PART 2	1" DIA. - 5 3/8 LONG	1
11	SPRING (1 3/8 LG.)	9/16 INSIDE DIA.	1
12	HINGE-BRASS	3/4 X 1	2
13	NAIL - FINISH	4 d	20

SIDE VIEW

FRONT VIEW

Tongue Drum

By Frank Pittman

The historical development of musical instruments such as the tongue drum actually began thousands of years ago. Early cultures in the Americas and Africa made instruments such as this from hollowed out log or limb sections. These early drums were called slit drums. Early people soon realized that different musical pitches could be obtained from objects of varying sizes and densities. Actually the modern day xylophone is based upon the same musical concept as the tongue drum.

Six musical pitches are possible with the tongue drum described in this article. The pitch of each tongue is changed by varying its length. The pitch could be changed further by changing the tongue thickness. It would be possible to tune each tongue to a specific pitch, but no attempt was made to be that precise since the instrument is basically a novelty item rather than a precise musical instrument.

MATERIALS

Materials used to construct the box and sound board (top) could vary. The dovetail box could be made from almost any convenient hardwood such as: cherry, maple (hard or soft), poplar, or birch. The type of material selected for the top will tend to change the tonal properties of the drum most, since tone is effected by density. Medium density hardwoods such as black walnut, cherry, and mahogany can be used. Higher density hardwoods such as East Indian rosewood, bubinga, or padauk could also be used with differing tonal effects. Black walnut produces clear mellow tones and was used to make the top of the drum pictured in this article.

It would be desirable if the wood used to make the top, was quarter-sawed to improve its stability. You will find, however, that it is difficult to obtain wide quartered pieces. The top could be made by gluing book-matched quartered pieces together like a guitar or violin top if you wanted to go to the trouble. The top of the drum shown in this article did not have a quartered top.

CONSTRUCTION

The construction of the drum is begun by making the dovetailed box which supports the top. The four pieces should be squared to width and length. It is important to add approximately 1/32'' extra length to the ends of each piece.

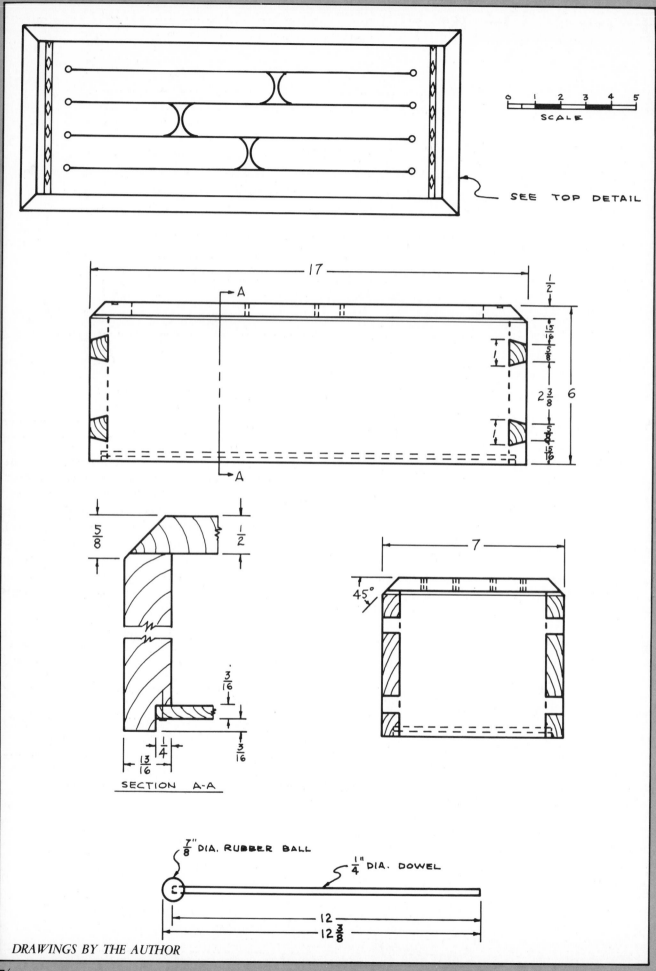

SEE TOP DETAIL

SCALE

17

SECTION A-A

45°

7

$\frac{7}{8}$" DIA. RUBBER BALL

$\frac{1}{4}$" DIA. DOWEL

12

$12\frac{3}{8}$

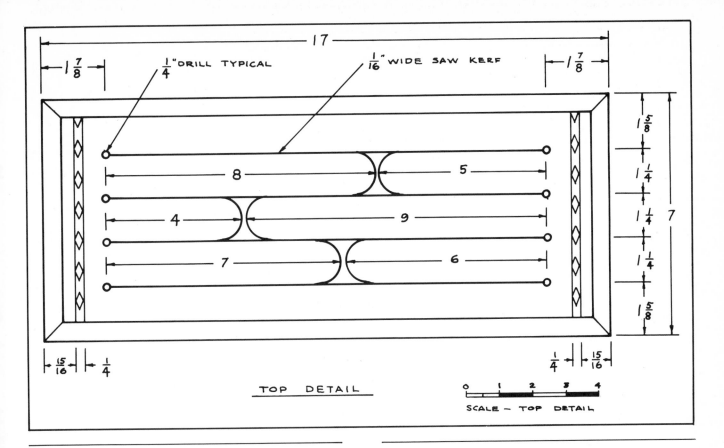

17

1 7/8   1/4"DRILL TYPICAL   1/16" WIDE SAW KERF   1 7/8

8   5

4   9

7   6

1 5/8
1 1/4
1 1/4
1 5/8

7

15/16   1/4   1/4   15/16

TOP DETAIL

0   1   2   3   4

SCALE – TOP DETAIL

The length dimensions shown in the bill of material include this extra length allowance.

The through dovetails can be hand cut or router cut if you have a jig similar to the Leigh dovetailing jig.

It is important in through dovetail construction that the pins extend past the tails on each corner as shown in Figure –1. This 1/32'' projection is sanded off after the box is glued up to produce a flush dovetailed corner.

After the dovetailed box has been glued and rough sanded, the rabbet is cut for the plywood bottom. This rabbet can be cut with a portable router and an 1/4'' x 1/2'' rabbeting bit.

The top of the drum is surfaced to thickness and squared to finished size. Next the holes and lines which form the tongues should be carefully laid out. Drill the eight 1/4'' holes through the piece. The slits (saw kerfs) between the holes can now be cut with a jig saw or a hand held sabre saw. These cuts should be as straight as possible. You may be able to follow the line freehand, however, it is also possible to set up a fence or guide block to help guarantee straightness. After the straight cuts are made, the curved ends of each tongue can be cut.

Inlay strips for the top can be obtained from a number of suppliers or you could make your own. Slots for the inlay strips should be cut with a portable router, straight bit, and guide. The inlay slots should be cut to a depth that would allow the inlay to extend slightly above the top surface. After the inlay strip is glued in place and allowed to dry overnight it should be sanded flush with the top surface.

The top can now be glued to the dovetailed box. It is important that this butt joint be a good one. It may be necessary to true up the edges of the top of the box with a plane to achieve a good fit. Several hand screw clamps or c-clamps should be used during this gluing procedure.

Forming the chamfer around the top of the drum is the next operation. This could be done in a variety of ways depending upon your available equipment. It could be hand planed, router cut, shaper cut (with a special fence set up), or cut on a table saw. You could actually use a moulding here instead of a chamfer if you desire.

The bottom is made next from 3/16'' plywood and cut to fit inside the router cut rabbet in the base of the box.

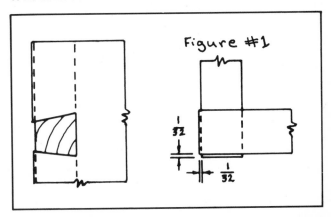

Figure #1

BILL OF MATERIALS

Quantity	Description	Wood	Dimensions T x W x L
1	Top	Walnut	½ x 7 x 17
2	Sides (long)	Hardwood	13/16 x 5½ x 17 1/16
2	Ends	Hardwood	13/16 x 5½ x 7 1/16
1	Bottom	Plywood	3/16 x 5 7/8 x 15 7/8

Inlay strip 1/32'' x ¼'' x 14'' total length

Dowel rods ¼'' x 12'', 2 each

HARDWARE:

Rubber bumpers with screws, approximately ½'' diameter, 4 each
Wood screws #5, 5/8'' flat head, 12 each
Rubber balls, approximately 7/8'' diameter, 2 each
Cloth or leather covering, approximately 18 square inches

FINISHING

The entire drum should be sanded through 220 on the outside surfaces in preparation for finishing. Several different finishes could produce satisfactory results on the drum but it is probably best to choose a penetrating oil finish since the drum is actually struck on the top when it is played. It is a good idea to coat the inside of the box with at least one coat of finish before attaching the bottom. This will help stabilize the wood.

After the finish has dried, the bottom can be installed with screws or nails and glue. Small rubber bumpers should be screwed to each corner of the base. These bumpers will lift the drum box slightly off of the surface on which it rests.

DRUM STICKS

The two drum sticks are made from 12 inch lengths of 1/4'' dowel and two small hard rubber balls. You should be able to find the rubber balls at a local toy counter. The balls are drilled and then glued to the end of the sticks. It is best to cover the ball with cloth or leather. (Figure −2.) The covering can be held in place with tightly wrapped rubber bands or string.

ABOUT THE AUTHOR

Frank Pittman is the graphics editor for **The American Woodworker**

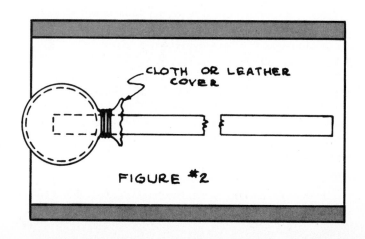

CLOTH OR LEATHER COVER

FIGURE #2

CIRCUS WAGON
A Fun Project For Father and Daughter

by Dennis R. Watson

When my daughter said she needed a place for her stuffed animal friends, we came up with the idea of a circus wagon. Of course, being a woodworker, I saw it slightly different; walnut for the frame, birch dowels for the bars, and maybe cherry trim. She rapidly informed me that a circus wagon was painted red and white. You just can't win an argument with an eight year old "woman". The design progressed rapidly, and final approval was quick to come, so "we" started to work.

The kids have always enjoyed helping me in the shop and this was going to be a father/daughter project. With any project such as this, you could make it faster by yourself, but you and your child lose that opportunity to do something together, and, of course, your child loses a valuable learning experience. The trick in making this a fun experience and not a frustrating one for the child is to plan ahead.

Young children, of course, are just developing eye and hand coordination, and some tasks are difficult for them. One way to minimize frustration is to design and use jigs or fixtures which will hold and align the parts or otherwise simplify the child's task. For example, when drilling the holes in the rails for the dowel bars, it would have been difficult for my daughter to hold the rail in position, align the bit, and drill the hole. However, a simple jig to hold the rail in place made the job easy; she only needed to align the bit then drill the hole. Safety is of the utmost concern; the jig allowed her to position the wood with the drill off, then with her hands, move safely away from the bit and drill the hole.

The construction of the circus wagon is pretty basic; the rail and stile construction of the side and end assemblies use a mortise and tenon joint. The side assembly is joined to the end assembly with a simple butt joint. Since the joint is mostly long grain to long grain, additional reinforcing with splines, dowels, etc., is not required.

We used red and white oak for the wagon because I had plenty of scrap pieces left from other projects, but most any hardwood or softwood would work just fine.

Photographs by the author

CIRCUS WAGON

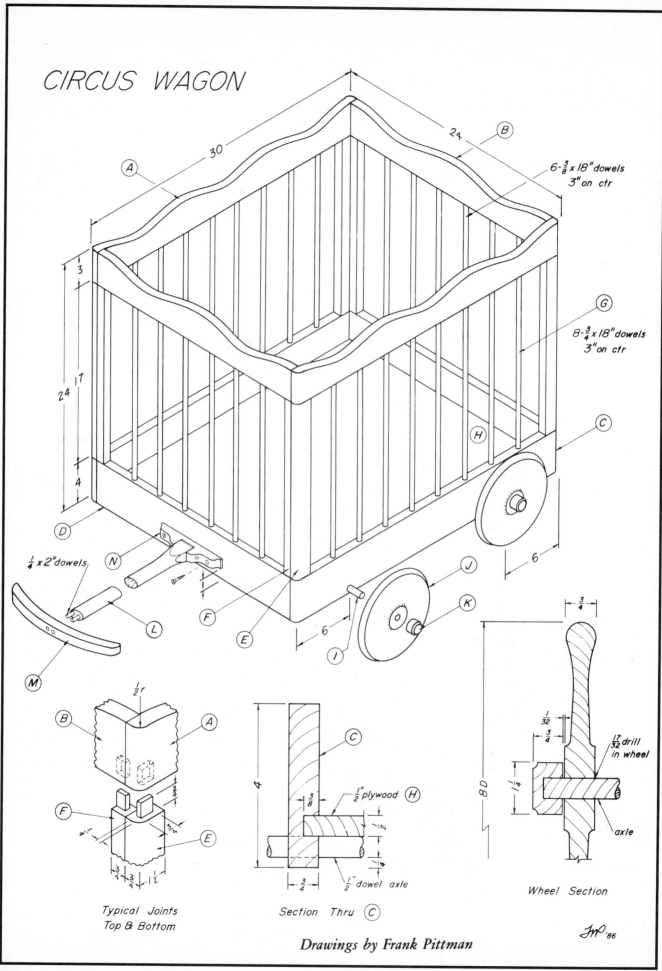

30

24

Ⓐ

Ⓑ

$6-\frac{3}{8} \times 18"$ dowels
3" on ctr

3

17

24

4

Ⓖ

$8-\frac{3}{4} \times 18"$ dowels
3" on ctr

Ⓗ

Ⓒ

Ⓓ

6

$\frac{1}{4} \times 2"$ dowels

Ⓝ

Ⓛ

Ⓕ

Ⓔ

Ⓙ

Ⓚ

Ⓜ

6

Ⓘ

$\frac{3}{4}$

Typical Joints
Top & Bottom

Ⓑ

Ⓐ

$\frac{1}{2}r$

$\frac{3}{4}$

Ⓕ

Ⓔ

$\frac{1}{4}$

$\frac{3}{4}$

$\frac{3}{4}$

$\frac{3}{4}$

$\frac{1}{2}$

Section Thru Ⓒ

4

Ⓒ

$\frac{3}{8}$

$\frac{1}{2}"$ plywood Ⓗ

$\frac{1}{2}$

$\frac{1}{4}$

$\frac{3}{4}$

$\frac{1}{2}"$ dowel axle

Wheel Section

$\frac{3}{4}$

8 D

$\frac{1}{32}$

$\frac{3}{4}$

$\frac{1}{4}$

$\frac{17}{32}$ drill in wheel

axle

Drawings by Frank Pittman

$\mathcal{JMP}$ '86

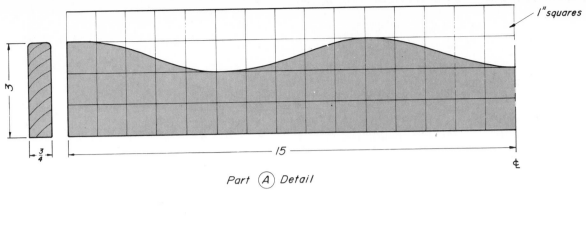

1" squares

3

3/4

15

Part (A) Detail

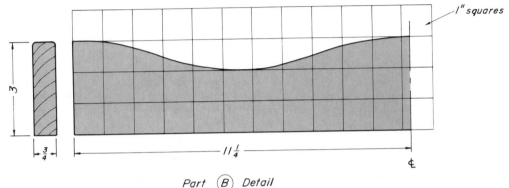

1" squares

3

3/4

11 1/4

Part (B) Detail

Tenons are easily and accurately cut on the table saw using the shop made jig in The American Woodworker, Vol. 1, No. 2. A quick acting, over center clamp has been added which holds the work securely and speeds up the process.

The first order of business is to rip the top rails 3″ wide. Cut the side rail (A) 30″ long and the end rail (B) 22½″ long. Rip the bottom rails 4″ wide and crosscut the side rail (C) and end rail (D) similar to the top rails. Rip the side stiles (E) 1½″ wide and the end stiles (F) ¾″ wide. Don't forget to allow 1½″ extra length for the tenons.

I've always found it best to cut the mortises first, then the tenons. There are numerous ways to cut the mortises, but I used a router with a ¼″ carbide straight cutter. A scrap piece of ¼″ plywood clamped to the base served as a guide. Feed the router so the cutter pulls the fence tightly against the work piece; take several light cuts and the mortise will turn out perfect.

Tenons are easily cut on the table saw using the tenoning jig shown in *The American Woodworker*, Vol. 1, No. 2. Cut them just a hair oversize then trim with a sharp chisel for a perfect fit. The tenons should be snug but not so tight you have to drive them in.

Up to now it has been pretty much an adult job, but now your child can start to help out. Clamp the four side rails together and lay out the location of the holes; center punch the holes. I used a brad point bit because it's easy to see the center of the bit and align the bit exactly over the center of the hole.

At what age should you allow your child to use the drill press? It depends, of course, on the maturity of the child. Some young children are mature enough to realize this is a potentially dangerous machine and must be treated with the utmost care; on the other hand, some teenagers are not mature enough. I allow my children to use some power tools but only under close supervision and obeying all the safety rules. There are, of course, some power tools such as the radial arm saw, table saw, jointer, etc. that I would never allow children to use.

Bandsaw the top end and side rails (A) and (B) to the shape staying just to the outside of the line. Remove the saw marks and finish up to the line with a spokeshave or rasp.

Final smoothing of the rails is done with a drum sander; this task is easier for a child to accomplish if the drum is chucked in a drill press rather than trying to hold and guide a portable drill.

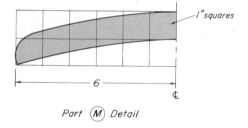

Part (M) Detail

1"squares

6

℄

After drilling all the holes, chamfer each hole slightly to ease the dowels in place during assembly.

Expand the design for the top rail to full size then band saw to shape. Stay just to the outside of the line, finish up to the line and remove the saw marks with a round bottom spokeshave. A drum sander mounted in a hand drill or drill press finishes the job.

If you are going to paint the wagon as we did, it's a good idea to paint the bars (G) and the inside edges of the rails before assembly. Dry assemble the sides and ends to make sure the joints pull up tight and all the dowels fit properly. Add glue, check for squareness and allow to dry overnight.

Run a ½" X 3/8" groove for the bottom (H). The groove runs the full length of the end assembly but should stop about 3/8" short on the side assembly.

Round over the top rails with a ¼" round over cutter with a pilot guide. On the inside

A shopmade jig clamped to the drill press holds the rail while my daughter, Carrie, drills the 3/8 inch holes for the bars (G).

of the sides, stop about 1" from the ends; finish rounding over the edge after assembly with a chisel and file.

Cut the plywood bottom to size and paint if desired. Dry fit the wagon together to make sure all the joints pull up tight and the wagon is square. Add glue and allow to dry overnight.

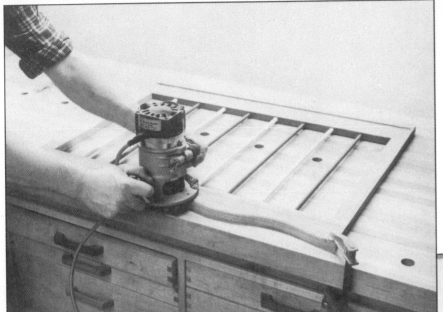

Round over the top edges of the top and side (A) and (B) with a ¼ inch round over cutter. Stop the cut about one inch from the ends on the inside of the side rail (A).

Carrie shaped the handle extension (L) with a spokeshave. The extension starts off rectangular and transitions to an elliptical shape. Carrie roughed it out and I finished it to final shape.

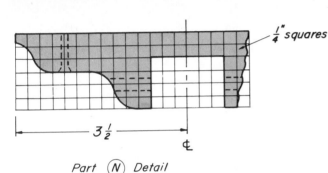

¼" squares

Part (N) Detail

3 ½

℄

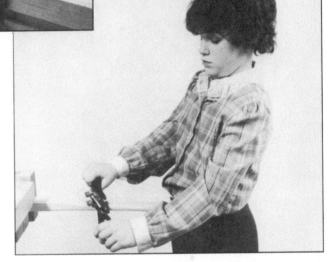

Part (L) Detail

¼ drill

3/4

7/16

end rounded for pivot clearance

1 ½

1

3

3

21

I wanted to add a little decoration to the wheels (J) so I turned them on the lathe. I scooped out the front and back face of the wheel leaving rounded edges on the outside and a small hub at the center. If you don't have a lathe, cut the wheel to shape on the band saw or with a saber saw, then round over the edges with a 3/8" round over cutter and pilot guide. Drill a 19/32" hole for the ½" dowel axle (I). Again, I turned the hubs (K) on the lathe, but you could also band saw to size and run a cove around the outer edge with a router.

Lay out the location of the axle then drill a ½" hole. Give the wagon a thorough sanding, check all pieces for splinters and round any sharp edges with sandpaper. Finish the wagon to suit your tastes or more exactly, your child's taste. If you didn't turn the wheels, scooping out the front and back face, you'll want to add a washer between the wheel and the side of the wagon to prevent rubbing. Glue the hub to the axle. A piece of wax paper between the hub and wheel will prevent the wheels from becoming glued to the axle.

Expand the squared drawing for the handle bracket (N) then band saw to shape staying just to the outside of the line; finish up with a file or drum sander chucked in a drill.

Cut the handle extension (L) 1½" wide and 21" long. The extension is rectangular where it attaches to the bracket and transitions to an elliptical cross section at the handle. Roughly shape the extension with a drawknife or spokeshave then finish up with a rasp or file.

Expand the squared drawing for the handle (M) then cut to shape. Attach the hand to the extension by drilling two ¼″ holes through the handle into the extension, add glue and drive two ¼″ X 2″ dowels in place. Trim the dowels then round over the edges with a ¼″ round over cutter.

"Fill with stuffed animals, and you are ready for the ringmaster."

Paint the bracket, extension, and handle then drill a ¼″ hole through the bracket and the extension. Redrill the extension with a 9/32″ bit to allow the handle to turn easily. Drive the dowel pin home (a little glue may be required on one end) then screw the handle assembly to the wagon using two no. 8 X 1½″ flat head brass screws. Fill with stuffed animals and you are ready for the ringmaster.

Mark the center of the wheel (J) while it is turning on the lathe. Then drill a 19/32 inch hole for the ½ inch dowel axle (I).

Mortises are easily and accurately cut in the rail using a plunge router and carbide straight cutter. A plywood block clamped to the base serves as a guide. Move the router so the bit pulls the fence tightly against the rail.

About The Author:

Dennis R. Watson is a contributing editor to The American Woodworker.

Circus Wagon

Cutting List

KEY	QTY.	SIZE	DESCRIPTION
A	2	¾ x 3 x 30	top side rail
B	2	¾ x 3 x 22½	top end rail
C	2	¾ x 4 x 30	bottom side rail
D	2	¾ x 4 x 22½	bottom end rail
E	4	¾ x 1½ x 18½	side stile
F	4	¾ x ¾ x 18½	end stile
G	28	3/8 x 18	dowel bars
H	1	½ x 23¼ x 29¼	plywood bottom
I	2	½ x 26½	dowel axles
J	4	¾ x 8 x 8	wheel
K	4	¾ x 1¼ x 1¼	hub
L	1	¾ x 1½ x 21	handle extension
M	1	¾ x 2 x 12	handle
N	1	¾ x 1½ x 7	bracket

Big Train Engine

by Jeff Armstrong

Photos by Jeff Armstrong

The Big Engine is precisely what it implies, it's one BIG train engine! We make this toy larger in scale than any of the rest of our toys with greater gluing surfaces for extra durability and turnings that are easier to execute. They are nearly indestructable. I think in the nine years of toy making we may have repaired two. For toddlers, it's simple to drill a hole in the front for a pull cord that can easily be removed later when a child becomes a more serious engineer.

The cab and the cab roof are walnut, the boiler is ash and we use oak for the base. The turnings can be any wood of your choice. Interestingly enough, we use furniture spindles cut down for the whistle, sand dome and headlight. While rummaging in the back of an old furniture spindle factory, I

came upon this giant stack of spindle seconds. All kinds of possibilities began occuring to me! I think by the end of the day I had almost a whole pickup load of spindles. These turnings are usually sycamore or hackberry, softer woods that machine well at high speeds. The smokestack, little people, wheels, axle pegs and the big ball for the pull cord all come from toy parts suppliers advertising in this magazine.

For this toy, the directions for construction will be divided in two parts: setups and general shop. This way all the heavy planing, ripping, jointing and crosscutting can easily be done at one time.

Begin setups for the bases by planing 6/4 or 8/4 oak (that's 1½″ or 2″) to 1¼″. If only the 8/4 material is available and the thought of turning all that fine wood into shavings is disturbing, an alternative would be to resaw a ½″ slab first,

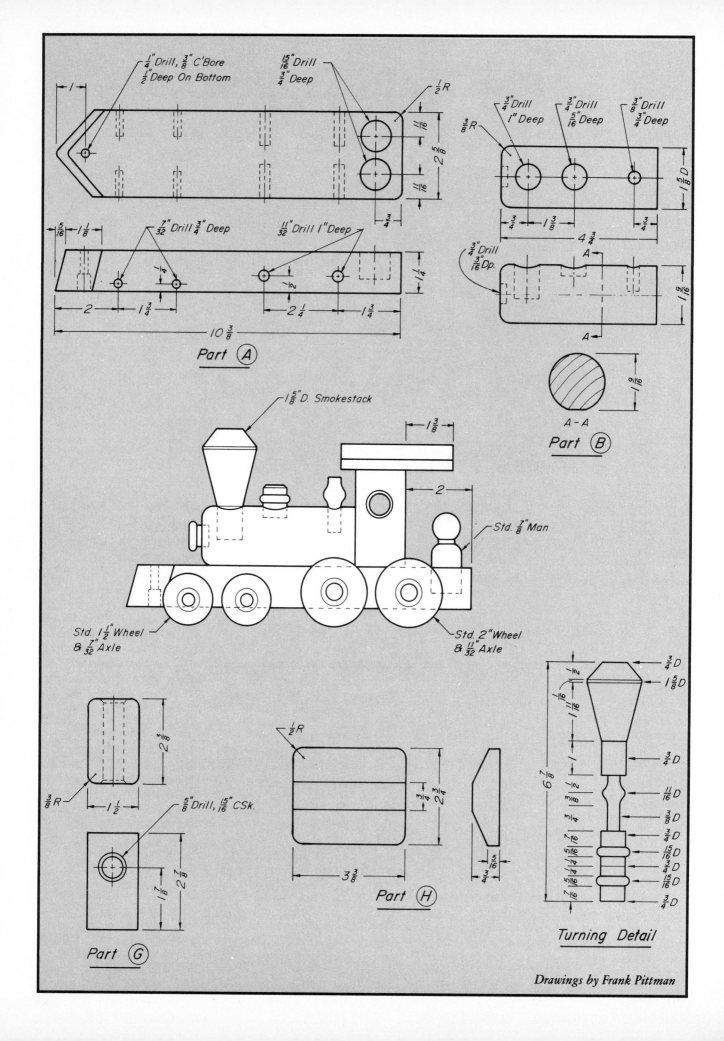

$\frac{1}{4}$" Drill, $\frac{3}{8}$" C'Bore $\frac{1}{2}$" Deep On Bottom

$\frac{15}{16}$" Drill $\frac{3}{4}$" Deep

$\frac{1}{2}$ R

$\frac{11}{16}$

$2\frac{5}{8}$

$\frac{11}{16}$

$\frac{3}{4}$

1

$\frac{5}{16}$ $1\frac{1}{8}$

$\frac{7}{32}$" Drill $\frac{3}{4}$" Deep

$\frac{11}{32}$" Drill 1" Deep

$\frac{1}{4}$

$\frac{1}{2}$

$1\frac{1}{4}$

2

$1\frac{3}{4}$

$2\frac{1}{4}$

$1\frac{3}{4}$

$10\frac{3}{8}$

Part Ⓐ

$\frac{3}{4}$" Drill 1" Deep

$\frac{3}{4}$" Drill $\frac{5}{16}$" Deep

$\frac{3}{8}$" Drill $\frac{3}{4}$" Deep

$\frac{3}{8}$ R

$1\frac{5}{8}$ D

$\frac{3}{4}$

$1\frac{3}{8}$

$\frac{3}{4}$

$4\frac{3}{4}$

$\frac{3}{4}$" Drill $\frac{3}{16}$" Dp.

A

$\frac{9}{16}$

A

$\frac{9}{16}$

A - A

Part Ⓑ

$1\frac{5}{8}$" D. Smokestack

$1\frac{3}{8}$

2

Std. $\frac{7}{8}$" Man

Std. $1\frac{1}{2}$" Wheel & $\frac{7}{32}$" Axle

Std. 2" Wheel & $\frac{11}{32}$" Axle

$2\frac{3}{8}$

$\frac{3}{8}$ R

$1\frac{1}{2}$

$\frac{5}{8}$" Drill, $\frac{15}{16}$" CSk.

$1\frac{7}{8}$

$2\frac{7}{8}$

Part Ⓖ

$\frac{1}{2}$ R

$\frac{3}{4}$

$2\frac{3}{4}$

$3\frac{3}{8}$

Part Ⓗ

$\frac{5}{16}$

$\frac{3}{4}$

$\frac{3}{4}$ D

$1\frac{5}{8}$ D

$\frac{1}{2}$

$\frac{1}{16}$

$\frac{11}{16}$

$\frac{3}{4}$ D

$6\frac{7}{8}$

1

$\frac{3}{8}$

$\frac{11}{16}$ D

$\frac{3}{4}$

$\frac{3}{8}$ D

$\frac{7}{16}$

$\frac{3}{4}$ D

$\frac{5}{16}$

$\frac{15}{16}$ D

$\frac{1}{4}$

$\frac{3}{4}$ D

$\frac{5}{16}$

$\frac{15}{16}$ D

$\frac{7}{16}$

$\frac{3}{4}$ D

Turning Detail

Drawings by Frank Pittman

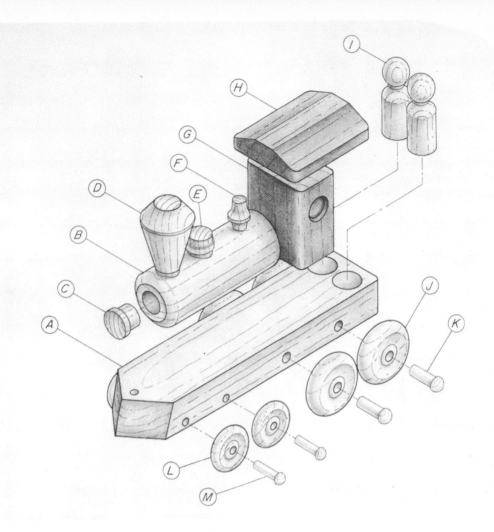

then plane the thicker of the two 1¼″. Rip to 2⅜″ then crosscut to 10½″. If the rip blade leaves a very rough cut and there is a jointer available, a very light pass on each side will save some sanding later on.

F For the cabs, plane 8/4 walnut 1½″. Rip to 2⅜″. The sides of this piece can also be jointed to save sanding. Be sure to plan this task before crosscutting since the 2⅞″ part will be much too small to joint. Crosscut 2⅞″.

To set up for the cab roof, begin by planing 4/4 or 5/4 walnut to ¼″. Rip a strip of 2¾″ at least a foot long to facilitate handling when cutting the bevels. Rip bevels 26 degrees leaving the 90 degree edge thickness ⁵⁄₁₆″ and a flat area on the top about ¾″. Crosscut this roof stock 3⅜″.

Crosscut the boiler stock to 4¾″ from 1⅝″ round closet rod or special lathe turned stock.

To begin the general shop work, drill the front axle holes with a ⁷⁄₃₂″ brad point ¾″ deep, ¼″ from the bottom edge. The first holes are located 2″ from the front edge. The second set of front wheels is 3¾″ from the front. Drill the rear axle holes with an ¹¹⁄₃₂″ brad point 1″ deep, ½″ from the bottom edge, 1¾″ and 4″ from the rear. From the drawing, mark the bandsaw cut location for the cow catcher bevel on the bottom front and the people hole locations on the top rear. From the same drawing, mark the corner curves at the rear if you prefer to band saw them instead of routing. Route the back corners with a ½″ radius router bit taking care to avoid tearout as

the cut is completed or band saw the curves just outside the mark. Now is a good time to add a pull cord hole if there is a toddler around. Counterbore a ⅜″ hole ½″ deep centered and 1″ from the front bottom edge, then drill the string hole with a ¼″ twist drill from the bottom all the way through. Band saw the cow catcher bevel with the table set at 12 degrees. Drill people holes as deep as possible (not all the way through!) with a ¹⁵⁄₁₆″ multi spur or brad point. Belt sand the cow catcher area with 120# taking care to keep the faces symmetrical. Belt sand the perimeter, top and bottom with 120#. Take care to keep the top very flat since this will be a glue joint later for the cab boiler assembly. Drum sand the perimeter and the bottom, breaking all edges with 150#.

Drill the cab window hole centered in the side and 1″ from the top edge with a ⅝″ brad point. Countersink this hole on both sides with the countersink running at a very high speed so that it has the tendency to burn as much as it cuts. This black burn will trim the window hole and finish it off. Route all four edges with a ⅜″ radius bit. Drum sand with 150# all the long grain faces. Sand lightly the two end grain faces if your belt sander sands true and flat for a glue joint. A pass on a sanding block or no sanding at all are alternatives.

To begin the cab roof, belt sand the bottom, end grain ends, and the top three faces with 120#. Knock the corners off with the ½″ radius router bit (slowly to minimize tearout), then drum sand with 150#.

Belt sand a flat area on the bottom of the boiler ½″ wide running its full length. Belt sand the rear of the boiler for a good glue joint with the cab. Route the front edge with a ⅜″ radius corner round avoiding the flat area by at least ¼″ on each side. The boiler assembly has several variables since the smokestack, boiler, whistle, sand dome, and head lights may be custom turned. The smokestacks can be ordered from toy parts suppliers. If different dimensioned turnings are used, just replace the boiler hole sizes with your own. Exotic wood accessories for the boiler will make a big engine really special. Begin by turning a spindle for one each, of the whistle, sand dome, smokestack and headlight. See turning detail for dimensions of our spindle. Finish sand on the lathe then band saw apart and drum sand with 150#, breaking edges that will show. Drill the smokestack hole with a ¾″ brad point 1″ deep centered on the top, ¾″ from the front face. Drill the headlight hole ¾″ in diameter and ³⁄₁₆″ deep centered in the front face. Next, drill the sand dome hole ¾″ in diameter and ⁵⁄₁₆″ deep, 2⅛″ from the front. Finally, drill the whistle hole ⅜″ in diameter and ¾″ deep, ¾″ from the rear edge. Drum sand with 150# excluding the bottom flat area and the back face to be joined to the cab.

If the big engine will be a pull toy, drill the 1½″ ball ¼″ all the way through.

Assembly for the Big Engine is simple and straightforward. To begin, glue the accessories in to all the holes, then glue the boiler assembly to the cab. Position the boiler in a vertical position and stand it upright on the cab until dry. Glue the roof to the cab centered side to side and with an overhang in the front of ½″. Belt sand the complete assembly flat on the bottom for the glue joint taking special care to sand precisely. Check the joint with the base often for a good fit. When the complete assembly is dry, fine sand by hand or flap sand the entire unit. To insure that all wheels roll, drill the axle peg holes out an extra ¹⁄₆₄″ for the middle four wheels only (¹⁷⁄₆₄″ for the small wheels and ²⁵⁄₆₄″ for the large wheels). Test fit all wheels on the base to be sure they all roll and to insure that the big engine is level. Assemble the 1½″ wheels to the base with small axle pegs. To finish up, glue the 2″ wheels with the larger axle pegs to the back four holes in the base. Use ⅛″ nylon cord for the pull cord and simply knot it to the ball.

Use the finish of your choice, or if the engine is for someone who likes the taste of walnut or oak, definitely apply

BILL OF MATERIAL

Code	Part	Quan.	T		W		L
A	Base	1	1¼″	x	2⅝″	x	10½″
B	Boiler	1	1⅝″ Dia.	x	4¾″		
C	Light	1	¹⁵⁄₁₆″ Dia.	x	¾″		
D	Smokestack	1	1⅝″ Dia.	x	¾″		
E	Sand Dome	1	¹⁵⁄₁₆″ Dia.	x	1″		
F	Whistle	1	¹¹⁄₁₆″ Dia.	x	1⅝″		
G	Cab	1	1½″	x	2⅜″	x	2⅞″
H	Roof	1	¾″	x	2¾″	x	3⅜″
I	People	2	⅞″ Standard				
J	Wheel	4	2″ Dia. Standard				
K	Axle	4	¹¹⁄₃₂″ Standard				
L	Wheel	4	1½″ Dia. Standard				
M	Axle	4	⁷⁄₃₂″ Standard				
N	Ball Pull	1	1½″ Dia. Standard				
O	Pull Cord	1	24″ Nylon Cord				

NOTE: Parts C, D, E, and F can be turned from a piece of stock 1¾″ x 9″

mineral oil. Add an engineer and a fireman and Big Toot is ready for the rails.

ABOUT THE AUTHOR:

Jeff Armstrong is a contributing editor to **The American Woodworker**

Fire Engine
by Jeff Armstrong

My wife, Nancy, made the very first fire engine eleven years ago for her grandfather, a retired fire chief. He was a collector of all kinds of fire station memorabilia and she wanted to give him something special. Since that time Nancy's toy fire engine has been through many changes, evolving to what it is today.

PHOTOGRAPH BY THE AUTHOR

The fire engine is made from cherry with the exception of the wheels, pegs, people, ladder crosspieces and nozzle. For the hose crosspieces we use padauk to bring out the red hues in the cherry. There is much potential for play with this toy; the ladder raises and swivels, hoses unroll and all the firemen can dismount to put out the fire.

Before Nancy and I finish assembling a toy I usually break away and begin what we call set-ups for the next toy, so all the lumber and rough parts are ready for general shop woodworking. Set-ups consist of processes like planing, ripping, crosscutting and jointing. These set up steps can be done for all the parts at one time or each part can be completed one at a time.

BASE

To begin, plane 1 inch cherry to 13 / 16". Rip 2 7 / 8", then crosscut 12½". At this point either joint the edges to remove the saw kerf or just edge sand with 120# . If all the set-ups are being done at this time, just set the base aside for edge sanding later.

Mark the axle hole locations on both edges of the base 2½" from the front and rear with a third pair of marks for the duals 4 7 / 8" from the rear of the base. These holes should be centered in the thickness dimension of the base. Drill 25 / 64" large axle peg holes 7 / 8" deep. We usually drill dowel and peg holes 1 / 64" oversize since they always seem to expand in size and also to give more room for

the glue. Drill nozzle holes 17 / 64" dia. 5" from the front 1 1 / 8" deep and centered in the thickness of the base. Drill the people hole 15 / 16" as deep as possible without going through 7 / 8" from the rear and centered. It is important to drill deep so the fireman doesn't fall out when going to a fire.

Sand the bottom and sides and break all the edges with 150#. Leave the top untouched at this time since it will be a joined face later.

CAB SIDES

Plane 1½" cherry as little as possible. It's okay to have a few rough spots since this material will be planed again after resawing. Rip a strip 3" then resaw right down the center. Plane to ½" taking care to orient the boards properly to reduce tearout. Crosscut two cab sides 3 1 / 8".

Mark a 1¼" radius curve on the front top corner of each side, then band saw. Drill 5 / 8" window holes 1" from the top of the cab, 1 3 / 8" apart and 7 / 8" from the front. Burn these holes with a dull countersink or use a sharp countersink at high speed.

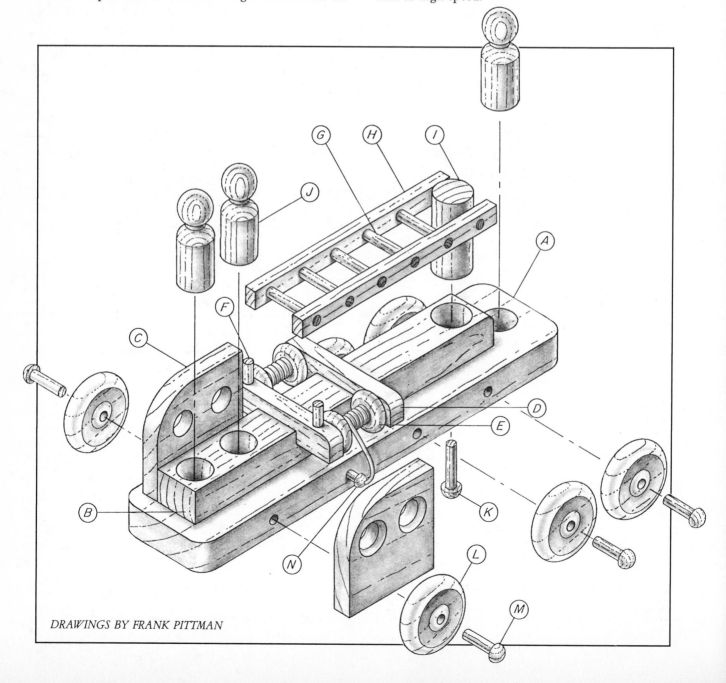

DRAWINGS BY FRANK PITTMAN

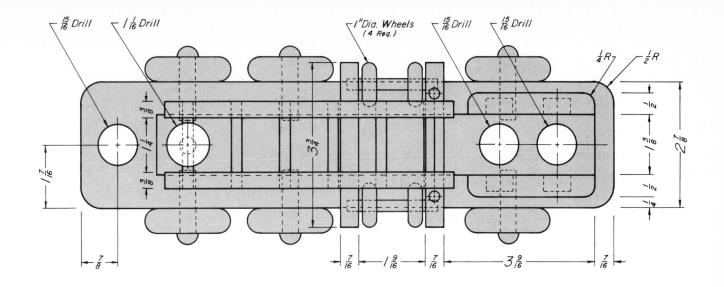

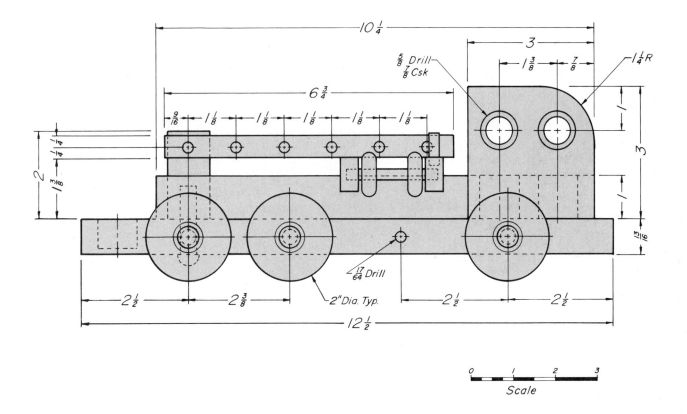

Scale

Edge sand the bandsawn curve to eliminate the saw kerf, then rout the outside face top, front and rear with a 3/8″ radius round over bit. Take care not to rout the bottom edge.

Drum sand the cab sides and perimeter with 150# except for the bottom edge. Leave the bottom edge sharp since it will be joined to the base later.

CENTER PIECE

Plane 1¼″ cherry to 1″, then rip 1½″. Crosscut 10 ¼″ and dado two grooves for the hose reel crosspieces 7/16″ wide and 3/8″ deep. These grooves should be 4″ and 6″ from the front, measured to the back edge of the groove. Next joint or belt sand the two sides to remove any tearout from the dado blades for a finished dimension of 1 3/8″.

Mark the two people holes 7/8″ and 2¼″ centered from

the front and drill 15/16″ all the way through. It's best when drilling through wood to drill almost through from one side then finish the hole from the other side. This method insures a crisp edge without chipping. Mark the ladder support hole ¾″ centered from the back edge and drill through 1 1/16″.

Sand the top with 150# rolling over the front and back edges. Next, sand the sides and break the edges only from the forward most groove to the back. It is important to leave the jointed sides unsanded where the cab halves will be assembled later.

LADDER

Plane 1¼″ cherry 1″ then rip 5/8″. Plane this strip ½″ and crosscut 6¾″. It is possible to just use ½″ scrap. If this is the case simply rip ½″ thick cherry 1″ and crosscut 6¾″.

89

Drill the ladder rung holes 17/64" through and 9/16" from each end 1 1/8" apart. Sand with 150# all faces and break all edges. Split two equal halves on the band saw. Crosscut on the band saw a 1/4" dowel 2 1/8" long for 6 rungs. Assemble 5 rungs into the two halves with the sanded sides inside. Take care to leave a 1" minimum distance between the two halves and leave the 6th rung out for assembly later.

Crosscut 1" dia. dowel 2" long and drill a 23/64" dia. hole 3/4" deep centered in the bottom. Drill a 17/64" dia. hole for the 6th rung 1 5/8" from the bottom side to side.

Sand with 150# the end grain of the top and bevel the edge. Assemble the ladder to the 1" dowel with the 6th rung, gluing only the ends of the ladder rung to the ladder sides, then sand rung ends and glue squeeze out off flush.

CROSSPIECES

Plane 1" padauk to 13/16" and rip 9/16". Plane the 9/16" dimension to fit the dado groove precisely, then crosscut 3¾".

Begin by drilling two 11/32" dia. holes as deep as possible ½" from each end of the two crosspieces to hold the dowel supports for the hose reels. These holes are drilled on the inside faces and centered. Then drill in only one of the crosspieces two 17/64" holes 11/16" from each end and 3/16" deep. Crosscut 2 pieces of 1/4" dowel 3/4" long then sand and bevel the end grain end. Sand the ends of the padauk and round over the top corners. Break all the edges that won't come into contact with the centerpiece, insuring an edge to edge crisp joint.

HOSE ASSEMBLY

To start, drill the centers of four 1" wheels 21/64". Band saw two pieces of 5/16" dowel 2" long. Bevel the ends lightly to keep the reels from sticking, then drill holes 9/64" through in the center for the hoses. To make the nozzles use small axle pegs or 1/4" dowel and drill hose holes 7/64" about ½" deep in the big ends.

ASSEMBLY

Glue the cab sides to the center piece. Test for fit first and, if necessary, flat sand the inside faces for an intimate joint. Be careful to use glue sparingly to minimize squeeze-out. After assembly set on a flat surface to dry. When dry, test fit to the base and flat sand with 120# if necessary. Glue centerpiece assembly to base, centered and 7/16" from the front edge and 7/16" from the leading edge of the back fireman hole.

To assemble the hose reels take the four 1" wheels and insert the 1/4" dowel into each pair. Put these reels together with the crosspieces (ladder keeper crosspiece in front), to test for fit and to determine precise wheel locations. Put just a spot of glue on the dowel, slide on the wheels and refit once again. Glue crosspiece grooves and set the whole assembly in these grooves on the center piece. Assemble 1/4" dowel ladder keepers in the forward cross member.

Drill the 3/8" dia. ladder swivel hole from both sides of the base and pin the complete ladder assembly with a large axle peg. From the top side drilling will be done through the swivel hole. Be sure not to peg the assembly too tight so the ladder can swivel freely.

Use 2" wheels and pin to the base with large axle pins. Before gluing, check for roll. If some wheels don't roll too well, drill out the center wheels 25/64".

Knot a 14" length of cord on the hose reel and glue on the nozzles to the other end. It helps to use a paper clip to push the cord into the nozzle.

Mineral oil, lacquer, Danish oil, or urethane—the choice is yours. After a coat of your favorite finish, the fire engine will be ready for that imaginery six alarm blaze!

ABOUT THE AUTHOR:

Jeff Armstrong and his wife Nancy own and operate Nancy's Toys in Huntsville, Arkansas. Jeff is a contributing editor to The American Woodworker.

BILL OF MATERIAL

CODE	PART	QUAN.	T x	W x	L
A	Base	1	13/16"	2⅞"	12½"
B	Center Piece	1	1"	1⅜"	10¼"
C	Cab Sides	2	½"	3"	3"
D	Cross Piece	2	7/16"	⅞"	3¾"
E	Hose Wheels	4	1" dia.		
F	Ladder Stop	2	¼" dia. dowel, ¾" long		
G	Ladder Rung	6	¼" dia. dowel, 2⅛" long		
H	Ladder Sides	2	½"	⅜"	6¾"
I	Ladder Support	1	1" dia. dowel, 2" long		
J	People	3	⅞" dia., 2⁵/₁₆" long		
K	Peg	1	½" dia. head, ⅜" dia. shaft		
L	Wheels	6	2" dia.		
M	Wheel Pegs	6	½" dia. head, ⅜" dia. shaft		
N	Hose Nozzle Peg	2	⅜" dia. head, ¼" dia. shaft		

Special Biplane
by Jeff Armstrong

My wife and I are toymakers who love wood and the processes used to shape it. Though many of the items we make are oftentimes considered as only toys, we think of them more as vehicles exhibiting the beauty of wood through simple and complex three dimensional forms.

The Special Biplane is one of the more challenging to make. It's my favorite since its design incorporates wonderful contours and an unsurpassed three dimensional form. In the special biplane, we use contrasting hardwoods to emphasize the shape of the individual parts. The fuselage is made from cherry and diagonal laminations of padauk with an insignia pattern of walnut dowels. The aerodynamic shaped wings are padauk and plugged to match the tail. Four struts connect the wings and are cross drilled with 1/8" dowels for strength. The padauk propeller is shaped just like the real ones with true pitch. Behind the propeller the walnut engine cowling is streamlined and inlaid with a padauk plug.

Fuselage

For the fuselage, begin with planed 1¾" cherry. Rip the cherry to 5½", then crosscut to 14". After the padauk stripes are laminated, this blank will be large enough for two bodies. It helps when clamping later to have a piece this large. Expand the short fuselage from Fig. 1 directly on the blank or make a pattern out of thin plywood. Place the first body with the tail section next to the end of the board on the bottom edge. This positioning will help later to cut the groove for the tail wing. Mark the locations for the two stripes ¾" apart at a 45 degree angle. Notice where the lines extend to the top of the board and position the second body tail section down and to the left and against the end of the board. *See Fig. 1.* Crosscut to the left of the left line and to the right of the right line so you have a ¾" cherry block separating the two stripes. To keep the board from slipping, use a backboard on the mitre gauge with nail or screw tips protruding about 1/16". It's important to make this cut without any slippage since this will be the glue joint for the padauk stripes.

Rip ½" thick padauk strips to 1 7/8". For the two body blanks you'll need two pieces 8½" long. Be sure the faces are very smooth. If necessary flap sand lightly to true them perfectly for the lamination.

Check all four end grain surfaces of the cherry for flatness and check the joints before gluing. Though the joint is long grain to end grain, in many years using it we've never had a problem. Clamping can be a little tricky since the pieces tend to slide. The easiest method is to use two bar or pipe clamps, one on each edge. Snug the bar or pipe against the edge to help maintain alignment. You can add extra clamps from bar to bar if necessary. A little slippage is okay.

After the glue is dry, plane both faces to 1 5/8". To straighten the edges rip again as little as needed. Expand the long body perimeter from the drawing. Be sure to position the tail section as close to the ends of the boards as possible. Stand the board on each end to dado the 7/16" groove for the tail wing 1 5/8" deep and 5/8" from the bottom edge of the fuselage.

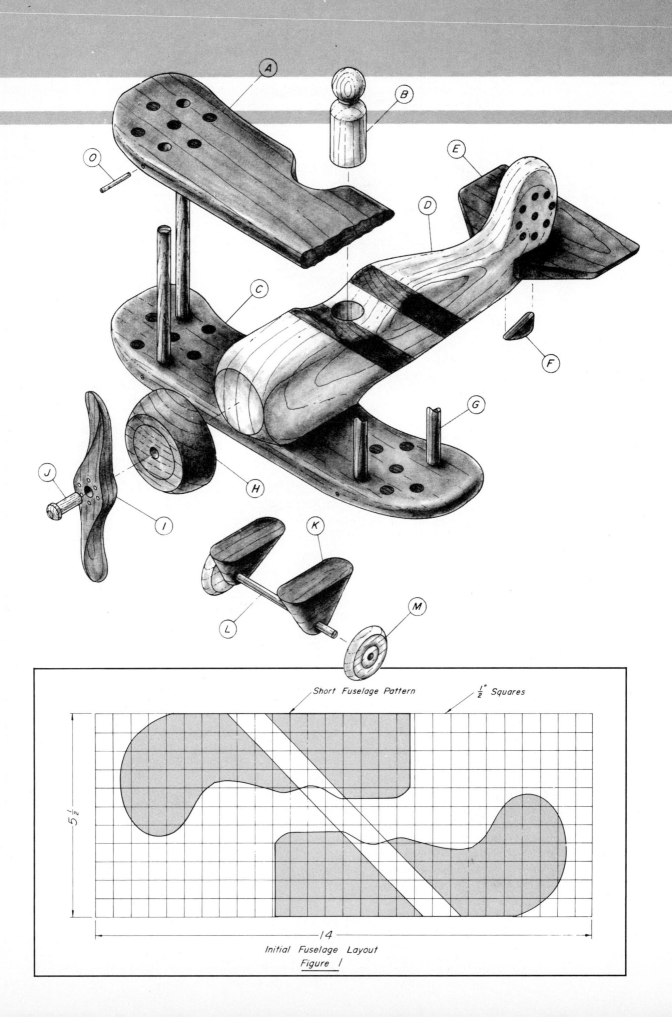

Short Fuselage Pattern

$\frac{1}{2}''$ Squares

$5\frac{1}{2}$

14

Initial Fuselage Layout
Figure 1

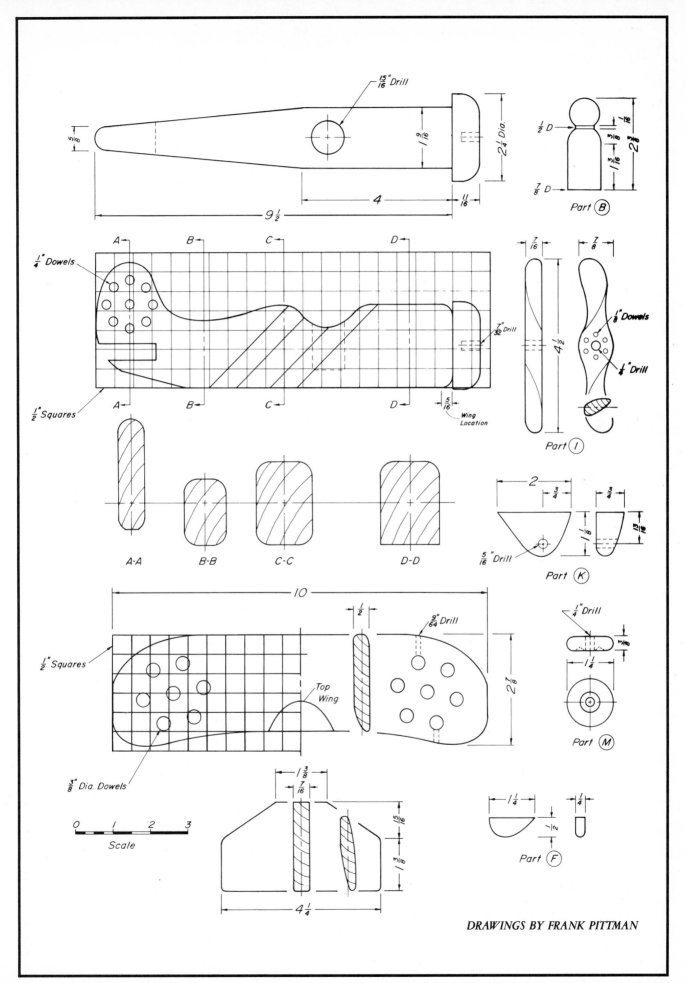

$\frac{15}{16}"$ Drill

$\frac{5}{8}$

$2\frac{1}{4}$ Dia.

$\frac{9}{16}$

$\frac{11}{16}$

4

$9\frac{1}{2}$

Part Ⓑ

$\frac{1}{2}$ D

$\frac{1}{16}$

$\frac{3}{8}$

$\frac{3}{16}$

$2\frac{3}{8}$

$\frac{7}{8}$ D

$\frac{1}{4}"$ Dowels

$\frac{1}{2}"$ Squares

A   B   C   D

$\frac{7}{32}"$ Drill

$\frac{5}{16}$

Wing Location

$\frac{7}{16}$

$\frac{7}{8}$

$4\frac{1}{2}$

$\frac{1}{8}"$ Dowels

$\frac{1}{4}"$ Drill

Part Ⓘ

A-A   B-B   C-C   D-D

2

$\frac{3}{4}$

$\frac{3}{4}$

$1\frac{1}{8}$

$\frac{13}{16}$

$\frac{5}{16}"$ Drill

Part Ⓚ

10

$\frac{1}{2}$

$\frac{9}{64}"$ Drill

$2\frac{1}{8}$

$\frac{1}{2}"$ Squares

Top Wing

$\frac{3}{8}"$ Dia. Dowels

$\frac{1}{4}"$ Drill

$1\frac{1}{4}$

$\frac{3}{8}$

Part Ⓜ

$1\frac{3}{8}$

$\frac{7}{16}$

$\frac{15}{16}$

$\frac{3}{8}$

$4\frac{1}{4}$

$1\frac{1}{4}$

$\frac{1}{4}$

$\frac{1}{2}$

Part Ⓕ

0   1   2   3

Scale

DRAWINGS BY FRANK PITTMAN

It may be necessary to crosscut a little from each end to get the slot for the tail wing deep enough. Finally, band saw the perimeter.

Use a compass to draw a 5/8″ radius circle centered in the tail section. Bisect the circle with eight even segments then drill the nine holes with a ¼″ brad point. If your walnut dowels run oversize, bake them or use a 17/64″ drill for your holes. Cut ¼″ walnut dowel 1 5/8″ long and plug holes.

To mark the tail section taper, extend two lines, one on each side of the body, but marked on the bottom edge from a point 5″ back from the tail end to a point 7/16″ from each outside edge at the rear. This will leave a rear tail thickness of ¾″. Bandsaw the taper then belt sand the tapered sides, the bottom and the front where the cowling goes. Drum sand to even up the perimeter. On the bottom edge where the wing assembly will go, mark off an area 2½″ wide and 3/8″ from the front. Rout the perimeter except the areas where the wing assembly and cowling will go with a ½″ round over bit with pilot bearing. It might be best to make a light cut first and leave out the second pass in the tail section where the body thickness is only ¾″ thick. Drill the pilot hole 15/16″ with a brad point or multi-spur. Drum sand, belt sand and flap sand to 220 grit rounding all the contours nicely.

Wing Assembly

To begin the wing assembly, start with ½″ thick padauk and rip to 3 1/8″. Crosscut two wings for each plane 10″ long. Expand the wing design and plug locations from the drawing. Remember the cockpit cutout is only on the top wing. Bandsaw the perimeter then belt sand to even things up. Check your dowel size and use a 25/64″ drill if they run over or drill the plug locations to 3/8″ if they run true. Bandsaw 20 walnut plugs 9/16″ long and glue in the holes. Be sure not to plug the holes where the struts will go. Belt sand both sides of both wings then drum sand the cockpit area. Next, mark the body position on the top of the bottom wing. Use a 3/8″ round over bit with a pilot and shape only the front bottom edges and the rear top edges of each wing. Don't route the cockpit area on the top wing or the area on the bottom wing where the body will join. Drum sand for final shaping and to gradually taper the routed edges into the wings. Finish sand the inside surfaces to 220 grit.

Bandsaw 3/8″ walnut dowels for the struts 3¾″ long. Glue into the strut holes assembling the two wings. It's best to let them protrude a bit so you can sand them perfectly flush with the wings. Drill 9/64″ holes about 1″ deep to cross pin the struts, then cut eight 1/8″ maple dowels. Glue in the dowels, sand flush and finish sand the wing assembly.

Tail Wing

For the tail wing, plane padauk approximately 7/16″ to fit snugly into the groove. Rip 2 3/8″ and crosscut 4¼″. Layout and bandsaw the perimeter. Make a couple of position marks exactly where the body will be located on the wing and belt sand tapers from the front corners on the bottom and from the rear corners on the top to give the wing aerodynamics. Take care not to sand into the area where the body will be joined to the wing. Break the edges with light sanding then finish sand.

Propeller

Use ½″ padauk 1″ wide and 4¾″ long to expand the prop pattern from the drawing. Be sure to mark the bolt locations. Bandsaw the perimeter then drill the bolt holes 9/64″ diameter and ¼″ deep. Drill the shaft center hole ¼″ all the way through. Bandsaw 1/8″ maple dowel a little longer than the hole is deep and glue. Use a drum sander or the round end of a belt sander to shape the pitch of the prop. Remove material from the front leading edges and from the back trailing edges of both sides. Sand the dowel flush then finish sand nice and smooth.

Engine Cowling

Plane a small piece of walnut to 11/16″ or belt sand a ¾″ piece. Use a 2½″ hole saw or bandsaw a 2¼″ circle for the cowling. Drill a 7/32″ hole in the center and mount the cowling on a pistol drill with a piece of all thread and nut. To shape the forward edge, spin the cowling against a belt sander. Next counterbore the face with a 1¼″ drill 7/16″ deep. For the insert use a 3/8″ thick piece of padauk and cut with a 1¼″ plug cutter. Another method is to cut the circle with the bandsaw over size and spin sand it to perfect dimension on the belt sander. Finish sand the face to 220 grit. After gluing the insert to the cowling, drill the shaft hole 7/32″ all the way through.

Landing Gear Assembly

Use ¾″ thick padauk and rip 1¼″. Turn this strip on edge and rip a bevel so on one side the thickness is 5/8″ and the other side remains the full ¾″. From the diagram (K), construct the landing gear shape and axle locations. Bandsaw the perimeter and round over the edges with the belt or drum sander. Drill the axle holes 5/16″. Bandsaw ¼″ walnut dowel 3 5/8″ long and assemble the landing gear with 1¼″ wheels. For the rear skid, plate shape a piece of ¼″ thick padauk like the drawing. *(F)*. Bandsaw the perimeter, round all edges with the drum sander and finish sand. Be sure the top edge is perfectly flat for the joint.

Final Assembly

Glue the engine cowling to the front of the fuselage taking care not to let the glue squeeze out where it will be visible. Glue the propellor to the engine cowling with a small (7/32″ dia. shaft) axle peg. Glue the tail wing in a slot at the rear of the fuselage. Sand a flat spot for the skid plate and glue it on. Make a couple of marks the width of the fuselage on the top of the bottom wing and center the wing assembly with glue. Double check for perfect center and 90 degree angle to the body before it dries. After the wing assembly dries, drill two 11/32″ holes for large axle pegs. Insert the pegs to reinforce the wing to body joint. Finally, glue on the landing gear assembly centering it on the bottom of the lower wing. Finish with tung oil, danish oil or your favorite recipe. All that is needed now is a 7/8″ dia. pilot person and the special biplane is ready to fly.

Wood people, axle pegs and wheels can be ordered from Cherry Tree Toys, Box 369-35, Belmont, Ohio.

SPECIAL BIPLANE BILL OF MATERIAL

Code					
D	Body	Cherry	1 3/4″	5 1/2″	14″
	Body stripes	Padauk	1/2″	1 7/8″	8 1/2″
A-C	Wings	Padauk	1/2″	3 1/8″	10″
E	Tail wing	Padauk	7/16″	2 3/8″	4 1/4″
H	Engine cowling	Walnut	11/16″	2 1/2″	2 1/2″
	Engine cowling insert	Padauk	3/8″	2″	2″
I	Propellor	Padauk	1/2″	1″	4 3/4″
K	Landing gear supports	Padauk	3/4″	1 1/4″	4 1/4″
F	Tail skid	Padauk	1/4″	1/2″	1 1/4″
	Body insignia	Walnut 1/4″ dowel 15″ long			
	Wing insignia	Walnut 3/8″ dowel 13″ long			
G	Wing struts	Walnut 3/8″ dowel 16″ long			
O	Wing strut crosspins	Maple 1/8″ dowel 9″ long			
L	Axle	Walnut 1/4″ dowel 3 5/8″ long			
	Propellor bolts	Maple 1/8″ dowel 2″ long			
M	Wheels	Maple 1 1/4″ diameter			
B	Wooden person	Maple 7/8″ diameter			

About the Author:

Jeff Armstrong and his wife Nancy own and operate Nancy's Toys in Huntsville, Arkansas. Jeff is a contributing editor to the American Woodworker.

by John A. Nelson

Storage Area
for a
Fire Extinguisher

Every kitchen should have a fire extinguisher close at hand just in case, but somehow a red fire extinguisher hanging over a kitchen stove is unsightly. If you keep it hidden away you probably couldn't find it in an emergency. This project provides an excellent place to store and hide your small auto-type fire extinguisher without taking away from your room decor. This project could also be used as a small wall shelf to store odds and ends. Just add two (or more) shelves to suit whatever you wish to store.

Simple butt joints have been used throughout this project. If you are an advanced woodworker you might wish to incorporate dado joints.

In the event you do not wish to make the letters, most wood suppliers sell 1″ high letters. The letters are rather simple and do not take too much time to make. Also, the wood will match better if you make your own letters.

Cut all parts to size per the given bill of materials.

Lay out a ½″ grid on a piece of paper or cardboard and draw out the top portion of the back, part 1. Take care to locate the centers of the six holes in the three hearts. Transfer this pattern, along with the six centers, to the wood. Locate and drill the six holes first, then cut out the three hearts. Cut the outside shape per your layout. Add the notches for the sides, part 2. Note the bottom portion of the back should be 4⅜″ as dimensioned.

Except for the ½″ × 4⅜″ notch in the top, part 3, all parts are simple rectangular pieces with 90 degree cuts.

To cut out the ³⁄₁₆″ recess for the letters in the door, part 5, make up a simple rectangular router guide and clamp it in place over the door. The required recess size, as dimensioned, is 1⅜″ × 3⅞″, ³⁄₁₆″ deep. The interior size of the guide is made up based on the diameter of the router bit you are using and the diameter, at the base, of your router. To calculate the required length of the guide opening, subtract the router bit diameter from the required recess length and add the router diameter at the base. To calculate the height of the guide opening, subtract the router bit diameter from the required recess height of the guide opening and subtract the router diameter at the base.

EXAMPLE:
(Using the given dimensions, a ⁷⁄₁₆″ diameter router bit size and a router base of 6″ diameter.)

Guide opening length

	3⅞″	Required recess length
MINUS	⁷⁄₁₆″	Router bit diameter
	3⁷⁄₁₆″	
PLUS	6	Router base diameter
	9⁷⁄₁₆″	Guide opening length

Guide opening height

	1⅜″	Required recess height
MINUS	⁷⁄₁₆″	Router bit diameter
	¹⁵⁄₁₆″	
PLUS	6	Router base width
	6¹⁵⁄₁₆″	Guide opening height

Thus, the inside dimensions of your router guide should be 9⁷⁄₁₆″ long and 6¹⁵⁄₁₆″ high. Set the router bit to a depth of ³⁄₁₆″ and route out the recess in the two given areas.

On a sheet of thin paper, draw a ¼″ grid and draw the letters per the illustration. Be sure to locate all centers of the ¼″ diameter holes and to lay out two letter "E's." Glue this paper to ¼″ thick material and carefully locate and drill out the ¼″ diameter holes. Cut all interior surfaces first and then cut out the outer shapes of the letters with the paper still glued to the wood. Sand all over.

ASSEMBLY—Glue the letters, part 8, to the door, part 5. Note the letters will extend out ¹⁄₁₆″. Let the letters set and then sand them down flush with the face of the door. Notch the door for the two hinges, part 6. Locate and drill a pilot hole for the knob, part 7.

Assemble the case keeping everything square. You may want to glue and clamp the case assembly together with the door temporarily in place as you know it will fit correctly.

FINISHING—This project can be either painted or stained. Because I was going to use mine in the kitchen as a place to store a small fire extinguisher, I painted mine red. Attach hinges and the brass knob.

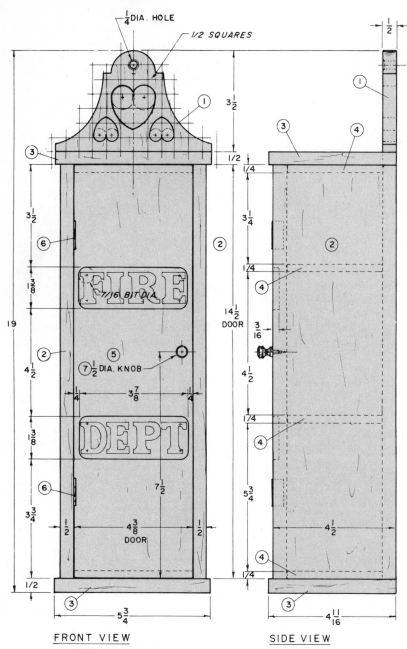

FRONT VIEW SIDE VIEW

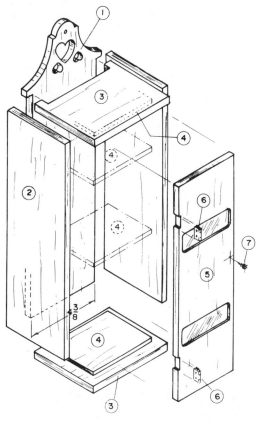

LETTERS

NO.	NAME	SIZE	REQ'D.
1	BACK	1/2 X 5 3/4 – 19 LG.	1
2	SIDE	1/2 X 4 1/2 – 14 1/2 LG.	2
3	BOTTOM / TOP	1/2 X 4 11/16 – 5 3/4 LG.	2
4	DOOR STOP (SHELF)	1/4 X 3 1/2 – 4 3/8 LG.	2
5	DOOR	1/2 X 4 3/8 – 14 1/2 LG.	1
6	HINGE – BRASS	1 X 3/4 SIZE	2
7	KNOB – BRASS	1/2 DIAMETER	1
8	LETTERS	1/4 X 1 1/16 – 13 LONG	1

PART NO 4 -- SHELF IS OPTIONAL -- ADD 2 IF REQ'D.

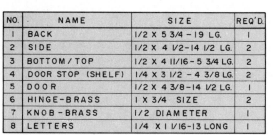